SONSHIP

Serge

New Growth Press

www.newgrowthpress.com

New Growth Press, Greensboro, NC 27404
SONSHIP
Third edition (2013 version).
Copyright © 2002 by Serge. All rights reserved.

All Scripture quotations, unless otherwise stated, are from the Holy Bible: New International Version®. (NIV®). Copyright ©1973, 1978, 1984 by International Bible Society. Used by permission of Zondervan Publishing House. All rights reserved.

The articles "Weak, Strong, Right, and Wrong," "Dead Man Walking," "Self-Forgetful Prayer," "I Can't Believe I Did That," and "Weakness Evangelism" were written by Serge staff.

ISBN 978-1-938267-79-6 (Print)
ISBN 978-1-939946-02-7 (eBook)

Cover Design: Faceoutstudio, faceoutstudio.com
Typesetting: Lisa Parnell, lparnell.com

Printed in Canada

24 23 22 21 20 19 18 17   3 4 5 6 7

CONTENTS

INTRODUCTION

Welcome to *Sonship*, a training tool to encourage you to greater faith, repentance, and love. The course is designed to promote ongoing renewal in your life, relationships, and ministry. Our prayer is that Christ will greatly bless and encourage you as you work through this course.

By way of introduction, we'll summarize the course in four points. These four points are foundational themes to the material, and you'll find the course often returning to them:

1. CHEER UP! THE GOSPEL IS FAR GREATER THAN YOU CAN IMAGINE!

The gospel is the best news we could ever hear. The gospel is about Jesus Christ and his power to transform our lives and relationships, communities, and ultimately, the nations. Through this gospel, we are freely given a new identity—an identity not based on race, social class, gender, a theological system, or a system of rules and regulations. Rather it is a new and perfect identity based solely on faith in Christ, an identity that defines every aspect of our lives. We are now forgiven, righteous, adopted, accepted, free, and heirs to everything that belongs to Christ. So even our sin, weakness, and failures do not define who we are. Because of this good news, we no longer have to hide from our sin and imagine that we have it all together. God knows and loves us as we are, not as we pretend to be.

Receiving and resting in the truths of the gospel translates into a Christian life of joy, peace, freedom, and love. Therefore, the gospel also gives us a new way to live and relate to other people. It frees us from sin's stranglehold on our lives, liberates our conscience, and releases us from living according to the principles of this world. Since our new identity and new way of life is based solely on faith, the gospel excludes all manner of boasting and arrogance. Everything we have has been given to us—thus it is called the gospel of God's grace (Acts 20:24). Moreover, this gospel has continual and daily applicability. It is not only relevant to us when we first believe, but continues to work in us and through us as we continue to believe. This continual life of faith visibly expresses itself in love (Galatians 5:6).

2. CHEER UP! YOU ARE WORSE THAN YOU THINK!

One of the great hindrances to Christian growth, healthy relationships, and strong communities is a life of pretense—pretending that we don't struggle with a multitude of sins, such as self-righteous attitudes, foul tempers, nagging anxieties, lustful looks, controlling and critical hearts, and a general belief that we are better than other people. Part of the good news of the gospel is that it can change our selfish desires to be right, look good, be in control, and gratify ourselves. Faith in the gospel transforms even good desires that have started to rule our lives and thus have gone out of bounds.

One chief prayer that speaks to our need is found in Psalm 139:23–24: "Search me, O God, and know my heart; test me and know my anxious thoughts. See if there is any offensive way in me, and lead me in the way everlasting." Because our sin is a block to intimacy with God and others, we need God's Spirit to show us our many fears and offensive ways. One way to promote this is to invite the insights of others, encouraging them to speak into our lives. The goal is that we repent and be led in the way of Jesus, and grow in our intimacy with him. Our goal is to live a life of repentance and faith—recognizing that when we live by unbelief, we are doing nothing less than trusting in something or someone other than Christ for life, happiness, security, respect, love, identity, fulfillment, and significance. Belief in the gospel tears down these false trusts in our lives, whether we're putting our faith in a system of rules or laws (legalism) or in something like food or sex (licentiousness).

Points 1 and 2 above work together in a cyclical fashion. On the one hand, none of us wants to look at our sin without having a firm foundation in the gospel, so it's essential to constantly saturate ourselves with the gospel, and grow in knowing its great riches. On the other hand, we'll have a small view of the gospel if we do not continually see the depths of our sin. The gospel cannot soak deeply into us unless it's addressing our ongoing need for it.

3. CHEER UP! GOD'S SPIRIT WORKS IN YOUR WEAKNESS!

In addition to our new identity, we have been given the Spirit, who is more than sufficient to lead, guide, and empower us in our new life. Often, we think that the great problem in our lives is that there is not enough power available to change our lives and relationships. There is, however, more than enough power available, for the power that raised Jesus from the dead is at work in us (Ephesians 1:19–20). Nevertheless, this power does not work automatically; it is at work in those who believe. So the Spirit works through repentance and faith. To live by faith is to live by the Spirit, who brings about the obedience God is looking for.

Furthermore, this power of the Spirit is made manifest in our lives through weakness (2 Corinthians 12:9; 13:4). We take the weak position when we have let go of our righteousness and strength, our claims to health and happiness, and our overarching claim to lordship over our lives. Thus, those who hold on to their righteousness and strength will find little power in their lives. Of course, this is further good news. God delights to use the weak and inadequate things of this world to accomplish his great plan for the world. With Paul, we can delight in weakness, for then we are strong, and God is glorified. The result is a wonderful freedom to forget about ourselves and stop wondering whether we have enough abilities, knowing that God uses and empowers the weak.

4. CHEER UP! GOD'S KINGDOM IS MORE WONDERFUL THAN YOU CAN IMAGINE!

The kingdom of God is the new and final age that began with the coming of Jesus. His kingdom is not part of the present age—an age where the flesh reigns; where people are divided, relationships are broken, and suspicion and competition predominate; where money, sex, and power are abused; where leaders are first and servants last; where behavior is controlled by law, and identity is defined by race, gender, or social standing; and where gifts and resources are used for the advancement of oneself. Rather, the kingdom of God is the new age. It is the age of the Spirit (Matthew 12:28). It is the age of righteousness, peace, and joy in the Holy Spirit (Romans 14:17). The kingdom of God is about the renewal, restoration, and reconciliation of all things, and God has made us a part of this great story of salvation.

It is about the restoration of relationships, justice, and equality; about freedom from every lord except Jesus; about reconciliation, forgiveness, and the defeat of Satan. It's about compassion for the poor and powerless, about helping those who are marginalized and rejected by society, and about using our gifts and resources for the advancement of others. It's about new communities and the transformation of society and culture, so that race, gender, and social class no longer define identity, nor are they used to control and divide. For Paul, to preach the gospel is to preach the kingdom, is to preach the whole counsel of God (Acts 20:24–27).

The gospel sums up the whole message of good news that he brought to the nations—particularly to the downtrodden and powerless. And since it is good news, our response to the message of the kingdom is to be one of repentance and faith (Mark 1:15).

USING THE SONSHIP MANUAL

There are three main parts to the course:

1. This manual
2. Audio lectures
3. A discipling relationship (the most important part of the course)

Each of the manual's sixteen lessons are divided into seven parts, which consistently follow the order listed below:

1. Lesson title
2. An introductory quote taken from the lecture
3. Lesson goals (in the right margin)
4. A reminder to listen to the lecture
5. An outline of the lecture, including any diagrams used, with space available to take comprehensive notes
6. Homework, consisting of:
   - A memory verse for each lesson (Note: memory verses for the entire course are included in Appendix C at the end of the manual.)
   - Approximately a dozen homework questions and various sections of teaching content (Teaching content is introduced by a large asterisk.)
   - A reading that relates to the topic of each lesson
7. A list of the various assignments to be checked off as you complete them

BEFORE THE COURSE BEGINS:

1. Recruit a prayer partner.

Prayer is essential, for God's work is not accomplished by simply taking a course, but rather through his Spirit in response to believing prayer. Commit yourself to praying, and to recruiting at least one prayer partner to pray for you throughout the duration of the course. Having a prayer partner is important, so choose a person who'll take this commitment seriously. Pick a person with whom you can communicate openly on a regular basis. Quite a few assignments will involve your prayer partner, and you'll need to update them after every lesson, letting them know how to specifically pray for you and how their prayers are being answered.

As a suggestion, when you get started, ask your prayer partner to pray Psalm 139:23–24 for you throughout the course: "Search me, O God, and know my heart; test me and know my anxious thoughts. See if there is any offensive way in me, and lead me in the way everlasting."

2. Read through the book of Galatians in Appendix A.

Reprinted from *The Message*, by Eugene Peterson, this translation of Paul's book refreshingly underscores many themes of this course.

FOR SMALL GROUPS—WHAT TO EXPECT

1. Expect struggle . . .

and don't be surprised to find that your group is a mixture of enthusiasm, hope, and honesty, along with indifference, anxiety, skepticism, guilt, and covering up. We're all people who really and truly need Jesus every day. So expect your group to be made up of people who wrestle with sin and have problems—like yourself!

2. Expect a group leader . . .

who desires to serve you, but who also needs Jesus as much as, and in some ways more than, you do. No leader should be on a pedestal, so expect that your group leader will have the freedom to share openly about his or her own weaknesses, struggles, and sins. Pray for your group leader regularly, and give your support and encouragement.

3. Expect the Holy Spirit . . .

to be the one ultimately responsible for your group's growth, and for the change in each person's life. Relax and trust him.

4. Expect your group's agenda to include . . .

an open, give-and-take discussion of the lecture, readings, and especially the homework questions and answers for that lesson. Also expect times of prayer at each gathering.

5. Expect confidentiality . . .

and be prepared to make a commitment that anything personal mentioned in your group must be kept in confidence, and not shared with others. Gossip will quickly destroy a group.

1

ORPHANS, OR CHILDREN OF GOD?

A believer is living as an "orphan" when he or she has somehow lost touch with the grace of God. In isolation from the promises, the orphan has developed a small view of Christ and a small view of the gospel. In contrast, a believer is living as a son or daughter when he or she is walking in faith, and living according to God's promises. Sons and daughters have a large Christ and a large gospel.

GOALS:

- To know that we are beloved, adopted children of the King
- To recognize that we are prone to trivialize the gospel, harden our hearts, and isolate ourselves from God and other people
- To understand that God invites us to confidently face our fears about life, and the worst things about ourselves, trusting solely in his righteousness and his promises as our Father

>>> LISTEN TO MESSAGE 1

MESSAGE OUTLINE

1. We are no longer slaves, but sons and daughters of God (Galatians 1:3–5; 4:4–7; 6:14).

2. What has happened to all your joy (Galatians 4:15)?

3. We trivialize the gospel when we trivialize our sin.

4. We are to live by faith in the promises of our heavenly Father (Galatians 4:4–7).

5. The way up is the way down (James 4:6).

HOMEWORK

Name: Due:

Memorize:

> But when the set time had fully come, God sent his Son, born of a woman, born under the law, to redeem those under the law, that we might receive adoption to sonship.
> —*Galatians 4:4–5*

Complete the following questions and exercises:

1. Complete the "Orphans, or Children of God?" exercise at the end of this session. Write your impressions below.

    "**Adoption is a family idea**, conceived in terms of love, and viewing God as father. In adoption, God takes us into His family and fellowship, and establishes us as His children and heirs. Closeness, affection and generosity are at the heart of the relationship. To be right with God the judge is a great thing, but to be loved and cared for by God the father is greater."
    —J. I. Packer, *Knowing God*, pages 187–88

2. Describe, in your own words, what it looks like for you to be like
    a spiritual orphan.

    I need to be write oops right! Can't take
    criticism. Sees the negative

3. From the "Orphans, or Children of God?" chart, list the five char-
    acteristics of a spiritual orphan that are most applicable to you.

    Need to be right
    Unable to tolerate criticism
    Tend to point out what is wrong
    Often dissatisfied with something
    Need to criticize others to feel right

4. Pick one of the characteristics you just chose, and describe a specific and recent example in your life that illustrates how you've responded like an orphan.

5. Describe a recent time when, by faith and humility, you responded like a son or daughter instead.

6. As you start this course, where would you like to see God change you? Write down at least three specific areas. In addition, ask your prayer partner to pray about these things.

We often think that a lack of joy is a result of our circumstances—irritating people in our life, lack of money, or bad health. The message, however, speaks a lot about joy and how it is rooted in who Christ is and what he has accomplished for us. When we discover a lack of joy within ourselves, the reasons may be varied. Like the Galatians, we may lack joy because we've forgotten what Christ has done for us, and have been abusing law by forcing, compelling, and judging others. We may lack joy because of fears that encompass our lives, such as fear of the future or fear of failure. We may also lack joy because we've failed, been exposed as a failure or fraud, or been attacked with criticism and condemnation.

7. Identify and describe an area of your life where you sense a lack of deep, spiritual joy. Why do you think you've lost this joy?

The message also addresses our need to seek approval from people. We do this in many different ways. We try to perform well to please family, friends, or coworkers. Or, we try hard to cover up our bad performances by concealing the whole truth. We may use laughter and humor so people will like us more. At times, we may also use flattery, subtle boasting, or fishing for compliments. Some of us withdraw and become quiet, while others act outgoing and important—all in order to "score approval points." Whatever the case, approval-seeking is an attempt to prove to ourselves, others, and even to God that we're okay.

8. Think of two recent examples when you've sought the approval of other people. What were the circumstances? What did you do?

9. How are we acting like spiritual orphans when we depend on the approval of others?

10. As you reflect honestly on your life, do you live as though you really believe God approves of you? Explain your answer; try to think of both positive and negative examples.

David writes in Psalm 139:23–24, "Search me, O God, and know my heart; test me and know my anxious thoughts. See if there is any offensive way in me, and lead me in the way everlasting." It is significant that in a psalm about intimacy with God, David ends with a request that God search out his fears and offensive ways. David realized that as he sought to experience the intimacy God created for us to enjoy with him, two obstacles in particular stood in the way: (1) his many fears, and (2) his offensive ways. Yet David could see neither his fears nor his offensive ways on his own. He needed the Holy Spirit to search him.

Likewise, our sins are like Post-it notes written on our backs—everyone else can see them, but we can't. The speaker states that the way to invite the Spirit's power into our lives is by first being severely honest about who we really are. However, if we cannot see what we're like, we need to ask God and invite others to speak into our lives, instead of responding with our usual defensiveness. To receive God's grace, we must be in a position to receive this grace—a position of humility (James 4:6).

11. Where do you think the power for spiritual transformation comes from? How do we access that power?

In preparation for Session 2:

Begin "The Tongue Assignment."

for one week, do not:	
gossip (or spread a bad report)	defend yourself
complain	boast
criticize	deceive others
blameshift (or make excuses)	

As you do this exercise, keep the following passages in mind:

"Do not let any unwholesome talk come out of your mouths, but only what is helpful for building others up according to their needs, that it may benefit those who listen" (Ephesians 4:29).

"All kinds of animals, birds, reptiles and creatures are being tamed and have been tamed by man, but no man can tame the tongue. It is a restless evil, full of deadly poison. With the tongue we praise our Lord and Father, and with it we curse men, who have been made in God's likeness" (James 3:7–9).

READ

My Father's Shirt

The Holy Spirit really dealt with my husband and me at the *Sonship Week* conference in answer to many prayers. I am seeing that as good as theology and teaching techniques are, it is the Holy Spirit alone who changes my heart. He tears down the idols and pride and replants the simplicity of faith in Christ. I realized that my greatest sin was unbelief and lightly esteeming all God has given me in Christ.

One day when I was very young, I saw my older sister hanging up my father's white business shirts on the clothesline to dry. I was suddenly filled with the urge to hang up one of my daddy's white shirts. He was my daddy too, and I was his daughter; I loved him in my childlike way and wanted to express it. I couldn't reach the clothesline—it was too high, but I saw a wheelbarrow in the yard and its handles were just the right height for me. I didn't notice how rusty it was and I rather joyfully clothes-pinned the wet shirt to the handles.

When my dad got home and saw the shirt on the wheelbarrow, he became very angry with me and punished me severely for ruining his shirt. I had not realized the impact that event and others like it had made on me. However, as I was repeatedly convicted during the *Sonship* conference for not believing God concerning his delight in me and in the gracious nature of my relationship with him, this memory returned to me. Now, you cannot hardly get through twenty-four hours of a *Sonship* conference without realizing that your own heart is as murderous as anyone else's—so I wasn't primarily focusing on only being the innocent victim of my father's cruel anger.

As I remembered these scenes from the past, I saw that through the years I had not believed that my Father in heaven was any different than my earthly father. I had not listened when he described himself. In short, I hadn't believed the gospel, that by faith in Christ and his perfect atoning sacrifice, he now loves me, and is forever for me and delighted in me. In Christ, he has made me beautiful and pleasing to him forever.

So the next morning I told our counselor that I thought I was beginning to understand. I told him the memory and said that I guess if the Father saw me standing next to the wheelbarrow with the ruined shirt on it, he would forget the shirt and hug me. "You still don't understand fully," Jeff said. "God would not overlook the shirt, but take it, put it on, and wear it to work. And when someone commented on the rust marks, he would say, 'Let me tell you about my little girl and how much she loves me.'" I was overwhelmed with that realization.

I am beginning to realize that my Christian life has been a continual effort to earn God's pleasure by "getting the shirts hung up right." God would answer if my prayer was right. God would smile upon me if my theology was correct. And since I knew how I had failed day by day in my works, I sort of snuck them up on the line and tried to be away when God got home, so to speak. Someone at the conference said something that seems to apply here. He said, "God will not despise the tainted love-gifts of the sinner who looks to Jesus." My entire Christian life had been oppressive. I did not know how to live day by day without an overwhelming sense of failure to perform up to what I thought God demanded. With that came a sense of God being disappointed and even disgusted with me. How overpowering it is now to realize that because of Christ, I can experience a daily freedom to move out into people's lives. I can love others. I can obey God with my heart because I don't fear that he will be furious with me if I "get the shirt a bit rusty." There is a freedom to love that I have not known since the moments before my father got home that day long ago.

I have been thinking of the "rusty shirt" and the parable of the talents. The two servants, who loved their master and trusted in his good will, served him energetically. They were not driven, but the very fact that they believed him to be what he was (faithful and generous) moved them to use the talents to the best of their ability. It was, however, the legalist—the one who viewed the master as a hard man—who hid his talent. My unbelief has led me to talent-burying. It is the fact that my Father delights even in rusty shirts that moves "this most flinty heart of mine" to really desire a life disciplined to seek him and find him, and by his power at work in me, to live a life of faith expressing itself in love.

An update: five years later

It is hard to believe that it has been five years since my husband and I attended the *Sonship* conference. Before we attended, I had worn myself out with trying to be a "godly" Christian mother and wife. I always felt that I had to be a better person than I was in order for God to be pleased with me. I had this constant weight of trying to live up to what Christ had done for me—so the Father would not be sorry he had saved me and made me his child. My husband and I tried hard to have a godly marriage and to be godly parents. In our minds, we had this ideal picture of what our family ought to look like. Reality was far different. Soon we were all becoming adversaries. My husband felt that my lack of respect and affection for him ruined his chances of achiev- ing a godly marriage. I felt that if he loved me more and led our family better, then I would be able to do my part in respecting and affirming him. The kids seemed bent on destroying any resolve in us to be patient, kind instructors. We resented them for that.

So, how has the *Sonship* training made a lasting impact on our lives? It showed us clearly the gospel message: that Christ died for sinners—like my husband, our children, and me. He paid the price to get eye level with us and embrace us where we are. The first immediate impact was to take the pressure off. My husband and I were able to repent and forgive each other for the critical spirits we had and the demands we had placed on each other. We could see each other as fellow, forgiven sinners. We also began to learn to accept our children and show them Jesus as the only one who saves us from our sins. The long-term effect has been crucial to us, as we have had to deal with the special needs of our children—physical, mental, and emotional.

Before *Sonship*, we thought we had to have our acts together. We had to know the right thing to do and be able to do it. What a relief to know that God meets us where we need him. I don't have to know, I can ask. I don't have to pretend to be strong; I can be weak and come to him. I can admit my weaknesses and my worst, cruel sins, and ask others to pray for our children and me. It is here that we have seen numerous answers to specific prayers born out of our weakness and our sinfulness. What a joy to know our needs are a window to God, not an obstacle that makes him disgusted with us. We still have much to learn, particularly about God's love for us in Jesus. We stumble instinctively. But we always know who to return to. And that has been as significant a change in us as our initial salvation.*

ORPHANS, OR CHILDREN OF GOD?

Read through the characteristics of an orphan in the left column below. Check off the tendencies you recognize in yourself and underline words or phrases that most apply to you.

In the right-hand column are the son/daughter counterparts to each orphan characteristic. Use the son/daughter descriptions as goals to reach for during the course, and beyond.

---

* Excerpt from a letter written by an attendee of the *Sonship Week* conference for pastors and their wives.

Orphans	Children of God
I will not leave you as orphans… (John 14:18)	But he has given us the Spirit of sonship and by him we cry, "Abba, Father!" (Romans 8:15)
☐ Feels alone. Lacks a vital daily intimacy with God. Is full of self-concern.	Has a growing assurance that "God is really *my* loving heavenly Father."
☐ Anxious over felt needs: relationships, money, health. "I'm all alone and nobody cares. I'm not a happy camper."	Trusts the Father and has a growing confidence in his loving care. Is being freed up from worry.
☐ Lives on a succeed/fail basis. Needs to "look good" and "be right." Is performance-oriented.	Learning to live in daily, conscious, partnership with God. Is not fearful.
☐ Feels condemned, guilty, and unworthy before God and others.	Feels loved, forgiven, and totally accepted because Christ's merit really clothes him.
☐ Has little faith, lots of fear, lots of faith in himself: "I've got to fix it."	Has a daily *working trust* in God's sovereign plan for her life as loving, wise, and best. Believes God is good.
☐ Labors under a sense of unlimited obligation. Tries too hard to please. Burns out.	Prayer is the first resort: "I'm going to ask my daddy first." Cries "Abba, Father!"
☐ Rebellious. Resists authority. Heart is hard. Is not easily teachable.	Has strength to be submissive. Has a soft (broken and contrite) heart. Is teachable.
☐ Defensive. Can't listen well. Bristles at the charge of being self-righteous (thus proving the point).	Open to criticism since she *consciously* stands in *Christ's* perfection, not her own. Is able to examine her unbelief.
☑ Needs to be right, safe, secure. Unwilling to fail. Unable to tolerate criticism. Can only "handle" praise.	Able to take risks and even fail, since his righteousness is in Christ. Needs no "record" to boast in, protect, or defend.
☐ Excessively self-confident or self-loathing. Discouraged, defeated. Lacks spiritual power.	Confident in Christ and encouraged because of the Holy Spirit's work in her.
☐ Tends toward an "I can do it my-self!" attitude. Is strong-willed, driven.	"I can do all things through *Christ* who gives me strength!"
☐ Unbelieving effort. Relies only on his gifts to get by in ministry.	Trusting *less* in self and more in the Holy Spirit—a daily, conscious, reliance.

CONTINUED »

Orphans	Children of God
I will not leave you as orphans... (John 14:18)	But he has given us the Spirit of sonship and by him we cry, "Abba, Father!" (Romans 8:15)
☐ Tends to be ungrateful. Is complaining, bitter. Has a critical spirit. Tears down others.	Relies on the Holy Spirit to guide the tongue. Praises, edifies, gives thanks, encourages.
☑ Tends to point out what is wrong. Is often dissatisfied about something.	Not blind to wrong, but chooses instead to focus on what is good and lovely.
☑ Gossips (confesses *other people's* sins). Needs to criticize others to feel right. Has the "gift of discernment."	Is able to freely confess his faults to others. Is finding that he is often wrong. Is eager to grow.
☐ Tends to compare himself with others—leading either to pride or depression.	Stands confidently in Christ. His self-worth comes from Jesus' righteousness, not his own.
☐ Feels powerless to defeat the flesh. Has no heart-victory over pet sins, yet has lost her sense of being a "big sinner."	As she rests in Christ, she is seeing more and more victory over the flesh. She sees herself as a "big sinner."
☐ Relatively prayerless. Prayer is a last resort. Prays sometimes in public, seldom in private.	Prayer is a vital part of the day, not confined to a quiet-time. Loves to talk to the Father.
☐ The Bible's promises of spiritual power and joy mock him. "What has happened to all your joy?"	God's promises of power and joy are beginning to describe him.
☐ Boasts. Points out her own accomplishments for fear that someone might overlook them.	Finds that Jesus is more and more the subject of her conversation. She boasts in her weaknesses.
☐ Concerned about building a record of deeds that needs noticing and defending.	Christ's righteousness is his "record" so he stands complete in him.
☐ Wishes people would see things her way. Needs to be in *control* of situations and other people.	Becoming Christ-controlled. Loves others in power of the Spirit, not in strength of her sinful nature.
☐ Looks for satisfaction in positions, possessions, or pacifiers (idols). Something other than Jesus makes him feel worthy, worthwhile, or justified.	Christ is his meat and drink. God truly satisfies his soul. "[A]nd having him, I desire nothing on earth."
☐ Lacks passion to share the gospel, since her Christian life is not really good news. Tends to be motivated by obligation or duty, not love.	Has a desire to see the lost come to know Jesus the way she does. Shares the gospel, even when not under the outward pressure of a program.

Check off the assignments you've completed:

☐ Listened to Message 1

☐ Recruited a prayer partner

☐ Memorized Galatians 4:4–5

☐ Completed the exercises

☐ Read "My Father's Shirt"

☐ Read all of Galatians (See Appendix A in the back of the manual.)

Session

2 THIRSTING FOR RIGHTEOUSNESS

We love to be in control. We're addicted to duty, order, our rights, our ways, and to outward performance. We might be outwardly moral, yet inside we're full of anxieties, fears, and guilt. As this session speaker puts it, "For years, I heard the words of the gospel, but I never heard the music."

GOALS:

- To see our tendency to drift away from the gospel into orphan-like living
- To discover areas in our lives where we try to build our own righteousness, particularly through the misuse of our tongues
- To see our need for Jesus every day, and our inability to change ourselves

>>> LISTEN TO MESSAGE 2

MESSAGE OUTLINE

1. "I am a recovering Pharisee" . . . "I heard the words of the gospel, but I didn't hear the music."

2. Latching on to (or developing "coping mechanisms" in response to) parental sin patterns

3. Family life

    a. Days of isolation—a move to Philadelphia

    b. 1975—Luther's preface to Galatians/"a caterpillar in a ring of fire"

    c. 1976—communion in Switzerland

    d. 1979—Uganda

e. "Rosemarie, you act like an orphan."

HOMEWORK

Name: Due:

Memorize:

> Because you are sons, God sent the Spirit of his Son into
> our hearts, the Spirit who calls out, "Abba, Father." So you
> are no longer a slave, but a son; and since you are a son,
> God has made you also an heir.
>
> —*Galatians 4:6–7*

Complete the following questions and exercises:

1. How well did you do the tongue assignment? Note some of the
    ways in which you failed. If you feel you had no failures, note why
    you think that is.

The tongue assignment helps to show us personally that we do need the gospel every day. It also demonstrates how quick we are to justify ourselves—how much we like to look good and be right. It shows how quickly we'll hurt others for the sake of our own righteousness. Our tongues reflect a far deeper reality. They show us that something far bigger lies beneath. "For out of the overflow of the heart the mouth speaks. The good man brings good things out of the good stored up in him, and the evil man brings evil things out of the evil stored up in him" (Matthew 12:34b–35). The tongue is a minute extension of the heart; it reveals what we believe and to whom we are committed. Suppose, for example, you looked out over the ocean and saw a tiny black speck moving back and forth on the water. From a distance, it does not look particularly large or dangerous. Yet if you were scuba-diving right next to it, you'd see what lies beneath the black speck—a huge killer shark! Our tongues are like those tiny fins—what lies beneath are our hearts that are deeply committed to our own righteousness.

2. Why is it so hard to keep the tongue assignment?

The misuse of our tongues shows our lack of trust in our heavenly Father. For example, excuse-making and blame-shifting show a victim mentality, and reveal my heart's attitude—not believing that my Father is in control and is protecting me. Therefore, I must fend for myself and solicit sympathetic allies to come to my aid. Likewise, complaining speech betrays the fact that I do not like how my Father is running my world, and that I can do better on my own. Boastful speech pays homage to my orphan successes: "Look at what *I* do (or did)." The implication is that I essentially did it on my own, without my Father. What comes off my tongue points to a deeper, more hideous reality in my heart—the unbelief and pride of a spiritual orphan.

3. Think about one of your tongue failures this week. How did it reveal the unbelieving orphan in you? Explain your answer.

Our tongues also show us how spiritually proud and self-righteous we are. For example, my critical tongue often reveals a heart that is sadly out of touch with how much grace, love, and forgiveness I have received. I know this because what's overflowing through my tongue is not love, but instead a spirit of being better and knowing better than others. I am right and they are wrong, and I need to point it out so everyone is clear about it. I complain, because I know that I am right and everyone else is wrong. Likewise, my instinctive defensiveness and inability to apologize sincerely and quickly demonstrates that I'm not really trusting Christ to be my reputation and righteousness. I must uphold my good record of performance before others. I need people to know that I'm better than they think (when in fact, I can safely say I'm actually *worse* than they think). These and other failures prove how easily I slip away from living out of the gospel.

4. Think again about one of your tongue failures. How does it reveal self-righteousness and self-justification in you?

Jeremiah 2:13 says, "My people have committed two sins: They have forsaken me, the spring of living water, and have dug their own cisterns, broken cisterns that cannot hold water." This is an excellent description of our lives when we misuse our tongues. When we gossip, complain, defend ourselves, boast, and criticize others, we forsake Christ who is the spring of living water and we start to dig our own wells. What drives all these sins is a heart that rejects Christ's righteousness and seeks to build its own. What drives my tongue is my desire to be right. What drives my boasting and critical spirit is a heart that has turned from God. Jesus' righteousness is not enough, and so I will use my tongue to get my worth, value, life, and righteousness.

5. What do you think your heart is looking for when you misuse your tongue? Why?

6. How do you think the truth of the gospel can transform the way you use your tongue? What would that look like to you, specifically?

The speaker talked about her love of control and addiction to duty, order, her rights, and outward performance. Quite often, our interaction with other people reveals how pervasive these things are in our own lives. The way we respond to people who don't fit into our world often shows us the unbelief in our hearts. God can use others to bring us to the end of our strength, draw us to himself, and enable us to taste again the riches of his grace and love.

7. How do you respond when God puts people in your life who don't fit into your plans, make you feel out of control, or upset your way of doing things?

8. Who or what, apart from Christ, do you expect or have expected to make you happy or fulfilled? Give one example.

The speaker also talked about sharing her heart with her rebellious daughter. She told her daughter about how she had been challenged about sin in her own life, and about the work God was now doing in her life.

9. Would you see this as a good model for relating to other people? How does sharing your weakness affect your relationships with others, particularly those close to you?

READ
On Received Righteousness

A paraphrase and abridgment from Martin Luther's preface to his commentary on Galatians. In the original work, Luther refers to the concept of Christ's righteousness given to us through faith as "passive righteousness." We've updated that language in this paraphrase by using the term "received righteousness"; however, the meaning remains the same.

It is necessary to teach continually this doctrine of the righteousness of faith, lest Satan bring the church once again into the doctrine of works and people's traditions. Because of enormous pressures that face us from every side—from Satan, our sinful nature, and numerous other temptations—this doctrine can never be taught and impressed on us enough. On the one hand, if this doctrine be lost, then everything is lost—truth, life, and salvation. On the other hand, where this doctrine is loved, then all good things flourish—genuine love for God, the glory of God, and the knowledge of all things necessary for Christian living.

The beauty of received righteousness
There are many types of righteousness in this world. However, the greatest type of righteousness is the righteousness of faith or received righteousness, which God through Christ gives to us, without our doing a thing. This wonderful righteousness is not political, ceremonial, or cultural righteousness. Neither does it have anything to do with our obedience to God's law. It has nothing to do with what we do or how hard we work. It is simply given to us as a gift, and we do nothing for it. Thus, it is called "received righteousness" because we do not have to labor for it. It is called the righteousness of faith because it is not righteousness that we work for, but righteousness we receive by faith.

This received righteousness is a mystery that someone who does not know Jesus cannot understand. In fact, Christians do not completely understand it and rarely take advantage of it in their daily lives. So we have to constantly teach it over and over again to others and repeat it to ourselves, because if we do not understand it and have it in our hearts, we will be defeated by our enemy and become ineffective and discouraged.

Received righteousness is the great comfort of the conscience and peace for the soul. For example, when we clearly see the law of God, we quickly see our sin. The evil in our lives comes to mind, it tears us apart, and we groan, "I cannot believe that I did that again. Lord, I promise I will not do it again." For when we are in trouble or our conscience bothers us, the devil likes to make us afraid by using the law, and he tries to lay on us the guilt of sin, our wicked past, the wrath and judgment of God, and eternal death to drive us to desperation, make us slaves to him and pluck us from Christ. Furthermore, he wants to set against us the parts of the gospel where Christ requires good deeds from us and with plain words threatens damnation to us if we do not do them.

This troubled conscience has no cure for desperation unless it takes hold of received righteousness. So when I see a person who is bruised and oppressed by the law, terrified with sin, and thirsting for relief, it is time to take the law and active righteousness out of his sight and show him the gospel of received righteousness which offers the promise of Christ, that he came for the suffering and sinners. Then this person is raised up and has renewed hope, now that she is no longer under law but under the gospel of grace.

Therefore, when there is any fear or our conscience is bothered, it is a sign that our received righteousness is out of sight and Christ is hidden. But when we truly see Christ, we have full and perfect joy and peace in the Lord, and we certainly think: "Although I am a sinner by the law, I do not despair. I do not die because Christ lives, who is both my righteousness and my everlasting life. Although I am a sinner in this life of mine as a child of Adam, I have another life, another righteousness above this life, which is in Christ."

How do we obtain this righteousness?

So do we do nothing? Do we not do any work to obtain this righteousness? I answer nothing at all. It is like this: the earth does not produce rain, nor is it able by its own power or work to get it. The earth simply receives it as a gift of God from above. It is the same with received righteousness. It is given to us by God without our deserving it or working for it. So look at what the earth is able to do to get the rain each season so that it can be fruitful, and we will see how much we are able in our own strength and works to do to get heavenly and eternal righteousness. We see we will never be able to attain it unless God himself, by the great gift of his Son, gives us Jesus' perfect record, and gives us Jesus' perfect righteousness. Thereby, as we have borne the image of the earthly Adam, we shall bear the image of heavenly Adam. We shall be new people in a new world, where there is no law, no sin, no remorse, or sting of conscience, no death, but perfect joy, righteousness, grace, peace, salvation, and glory.

The obedience that flows from received righteousness

Paul diligently sets out in this letter to teach us, to comfort us, and to keep us constantly aware of this great Christian righteousness. For if the truth of our being justified by Christ alone is lost, then all Christian truths are lost. There is no middle ground between "received" and "earned" righteousness. The person who wanders away from received righteousness has no other choice but live by earned righteousness. If he does not depend on the work of Christ, he must depend on his own work. So we must teach and continually repeat the truth of this received" or "Christian" righteousness so that Christians continue to hold to it and never confuse it with earned righteousness. On this truth, the church is built and has its being.

Now, when I have this righteousness reigning in my heart, I descend from heaven like rain making the earth fruitful, that is to say, I enter into a new kingdom and I do "good works" whenever and however I get the opportunity. In conclusion, whoever is convicted that Christ is his only righteousness, does not only do his work cheerfully, gladly and well, but also, if necessary, submits to all kinds of burdens and sufferings in this life with love because he knows this is God's will, and that God is pleased by his obedience.

Check off the assignments you've completed:

☐ Listened to Message 2   ☐ Read "On Received Righteousness"
☐ Memorized Galatians 4:6–7 ☐ Updated my prayer partner
☐ Completed the exercises

Session

3 RECEIVED RIGHTEOUSNESS

Why does the church have a problem with honesty? If we must rely on what we can do to make ourselves approved by God, we cannot look at our sin. In fact, we have a stake in *not* seeing it. It's to our "benefit" to not be *too* honest. It is too threatening. However, it is the righteousness of Christ credited to our account (i.e., received righteousness) that frees us to be honest about our struggles and sins, and to not be crushed by them. Unless we hold on to this by faith, honesty is just too hard and frightening. Hypocrisy is then just a small step away.

GOALS:

- To understand the concept of "received righteousness"
- To let the truth of justification by faith impact our lives in practical and specific ways
- To see how our justification frees us to be honest about ourselves

>>> LISTEN TO MESSAGE 3

MESSAGE OUTLINE

1. Introduction: the tongue assignment

2. Two diagnostic questions . . . and two more

3. Two kinds of righteousness

   a. Passive/received righteousness

    b. Active/earned righteousness

4. Foundations for real change

    a. Confidence in the righteousness of Christ equips us to be honest

    b. The present value of the blood of Christ: we are perfect forever (Hebrews 10:14)!

HOMEWORK

Name: Due:

Memorize:

For in the gospel a righteousness from God is revealed, a righteousness that is by faith from first to last, just as it is written: "The righteous will live by faith."

—Romans 1:17

Complete the following questions and exercises:

1. Off the top of your head, write out your own definition of justification by faith.

2. Of the statements below, which option, A or B, is true? Circle the appropriate letter to indicate your choice.

   1   **A**   Justification is a single act of God for us.

        B   Justification is an ongoing work of God in us.

   2   **A**   Justification means "to make righteous."

        B   Justification means "to declare righteous."

   3   **A**   Faith plus works = salvation (justification).

        B   Faith in Christ alone = salvation (justification) plus works.

   4   **A**   Imputation (crediting) means not counting us guilty for our sins and counting us as righteous as Christ.

        B   Imputation means only not counting us guilty.

   5   **A**   The nature of faith is to receive Christ.

        B   The nature of love is to receive Christ.

   6   **A**   Faith alone justifies by uniting us to Christ.

        B   Faith alone with baptism justifies by uniting us to Christ.

   7   **A**   Justification frees us from all responsibility to obey the law of God.

        B   Justification is a declaration that we are righteous and a pardon of our sins, which sets us free to obey God's law by faith.

3. Look at the answer key found at the end of these exercises. Compare your choices with the answers there, and make any corrections necessary. Also, note below any important elements you may have left out of your definition of justification by faith.

4. Now, rewrite your definition of justification by faith. Be sure to include the following key elements, in your own words:
    - **Something is taken away.** Christ's substitutionary sacrifice (atonement) secures for us the forgiveness of past, present, and future sins.
    - **Something is given.** Christ's perfect obedience to the law (righteousness) is credited to us as our own righteousness.
    - **This is a once-for-all-time legal act.**
    - **It is received by grace** through the instrument of faith alone, and is not tied to our performance.

What is faith? Faith is merely an instrument, an empty hand. It is receiving what only God can give us. Faith is the conduit, pipe, or channel through which we receive the gospel. Faith is the electrical cord in your home—it is not the power, but rather the instrument through which electrical power travels. Similarly, faith is the instrument through which the great power of the Holy Spirit works. All the blessings of the gospel come into our hearts through the instrument of faith. Faith is the instrument through which we receive forgiveness, justification, and Christ's righteousness.

5. Describe, in your own words, what faith is.

The Heidelberg Catechism says in question 60:

Q. How are you right with God?
A. Only by true faith in Jesus Christ.

Even though my conscience accuses me of having grievously sinned against all God's commandments and of never having kept any of them, and even though I am still inclined toward all evil, nevertheless, without my deserving it at all, out of sheer grace, God grants and credits to me the perfect satisfaction, righteousness, and holiness of Christ, as if I had never sinned nor been a sinner, as if I had been as perfectly obedient as Christ was obedient for me. All I need to do is accept this gift of God with a believing heart [1975 translation].

6. Describe the good news of Jesus Christ, in your own words. Why is it so good for *you* to have the perfect righteousness of Christ credited to your account?

We often come up with certain rules or laws, believing that if we keep them we are more "right" before God. From there, it's only a small step before we start using these rules or laws to judge other people based on *their* performance. The rules we make for ourselves are often good things. However, we often abuse them. For example, as we struggle with the desire to be in control of our lives, we erect laws that try to maintain that control. These laws could be as simple as, "Don't cut me off on the road," or "The house has to be kept tidy." When people break these laws, we feel we're losing control and that people don't respect us. Moreover, we feel that we're right and they're wrong. The usual result is anger, whereby we try to retake control of the situation and show just how right we are. Thus, instead of the law being used to help us love other people, we use it against other people.

7. What's one rule you've made for yourself and others that makes you feel good when kept, but leaves you irritated or depressed when it's broken?

8. How has your rule-keeping given you a sense of righteousness? How does being mastered by this rule keep you from genuinely loving other people?

9. Think of an example, such as describing a time when you frightened someone with your intensity, or hurt or distanced your spouse or close friend because of your desire to be right. Why do you think your desire to be right is so much stronger in these situations than your desire to be forgiven?

10. How would getting your sense of righteousness from Jesus instead affect how you respond in those situations? What other areas of your life would change? Be specific.

11. How do you think God views you right now? What is his attitude toward you?

12. Think of someone close to you, such as a friend, spouse, or child. How would you describe your love for that person? How does it compare and contrast with your perception of *God's* love for *you*?

13. What can you do to change God's opinion of you? Explain your answer.

READ

The Weak, Strong, Right, and Wrong

The great paradox of the kingdom concerns the weak, strong, right, and wrong. The paradox is this: Those who are considered strong and right are weak and wrong. And those who are considered weak and wrong are right and strong. What does this mean? There are two great drives in our hearts: the one to be strong, the other to be right.

We love to be strong. We love the strength that comes from youth, money, beauty, intelligence, prestigious work, good health, or fame. We work hard to be in positions of strength in our relationships through manipulation, control, intimidation, and anger. We try to control our lives, homes, families, and friends (and enemies!) to maintain this supposed position of strength. We hate to take the weak position, the position of powerlessness.

We also love to be right. Every day, as soon as we wake up, our hearts are seeking new ways to be justified. We long to think better of ourselves, and we long for others to think well of us. We work hard to keep our reputation and are quick to put someone down in order to improve our reputation. As the writer of Ecclesiastes says, "I saw that all labor and all achievement spring from man's envy of his neighbor" (Ecclesiastes 4:4). We work hard to be better and look better than everyone else.

Nevertheless, as we place ourselves in the position of strength and "rightness," we're actually distancing ourselves from grace and from the Spirit's power in our lives. Jesus' power is made perfect in weakness (2 Corinthians 12:9). By taking the position of being right and strong, we also distance ourselves from other people, especially those close to us.

"I used to be conceited, but now I'm perfect." I'm right about my kids, my spouse, and my work. I'm right about how my home should be run. I'm right about how the church should function. I'm right about my enemies, and know why they are so wrong. I study hard to be right about all sorts of things. What do you think it's like to *live* with me?

Because I am right:

- I don't listen. (Why listen when I already know the *right* answer?)
- I complain. (Other people have it wrong; God is wrong. I know what's best and *right*.)
- I boast. (It feels great for others to see how *right* I am about all sorts of things.)
- I defend myself. (Don't try and undermine my edifice of *right*eousness, which I've been building for many years.)
- I attack and accuse. (You're not as *right* as you think you are.)
- I am harsh with others. (They just don't have it together. There's something *wrong* with them.)
- I am critical. (People need my helpful *correction* for their improvement.)
- I gossip. (I'm *right* about other people and their problems.)

It comes naturally to be strong and right. Yet the gospel says there is only one who is strong and right—Jesus. So it is only through the gospel that I come to realize that I am in fact weak and wrong. Thus, the place I don't want to be is the place I need to be. The truly powerful place is the place where I give up my power, "for when I am weak, then I am strong" (2 Corinthians 12:10). The place of righteousness is the place where I give up my own righteousness, and receive by faith the righteousness of Christ.

"I'm not opinionated. I'm just always right!" There was an article in the *Philadelphia Inquirer* on how to say you are sorry and still be right. The article described how, once you realize you don't have to make yourself wrong to deliver an apology, you'll feel a new power. I devoured the article! It's just what I wanted to hear. How to appear to be contrite and still be right—what a great position to be in! Finally, here's a way to look even more right—doubly right! Seriously, though, our hearts look for ways to be right without appearing arrogant at the same time. We know that outright arrogance usually makes us look bad, so we think of ways to stay right and look good in the process.

"O Lord, it's hard to be humble when you're perfect in every way." Significantly, in the garden of Eden, following the fall, the first thing that Adam and Eve did is to seek their own righteousness by complaining, defending, and attacking. The first inclination of their fallen hearts was to hide, blame, accuse, and deceive. They would stop at nothing, including blaming God. Adam wasted no time telling God that the whole problem developed because of "the woman you put here with me" (Genesis 3:12). Neither did the quest for righteousness stop there. The history of Israel is the history of a nation's attempt to establish its own righteousness. One unifying characteristic of world religions is the desire to be right before their gods. It should be no surprise, therefore, that our great struggle in the Christian life is the struggle for righteousness. The battle is over whether we will live out of the righteousness of Christ, rather than building our own.

"I'm so perfect, it even scares me!" Through the gospel, we are declared perfect and righteous. Faced with this wonderful news, the question invariably arises, "What about obedience?" If we're already perfect, why bother making every effort to love others? The fear is that the righteousness of Christ that we receive by faith will lead to our doing nothing. It is not hard, however, to show that this is untrue. Believing that God loves you does not lead to apathy—a mentality that says "Oh, it doesn't matter what I do, because God loves me." Rather, if we genuinely believe God's love, it compels us to love others (2 Corinthians 5:14). Similarly, with received righteousness, the righteousness of Christ compels us to love people, not to gossip, complain, defend, criticize, or boast. It gives us the foundation and motivation for genuine obedience. Note the following:

- The foundation of received righteousness leads to genuine obedience.
- "Earned" righteousness leads to self-centeredness and disobedience.

In other words, if you base your life on whom Christ is and what he has done for you, you'll find yourself actively loving other people. If you base your life on what you're doing and how well you're doing it, you'll fail to love others (since you'll be focused on yourself). One approach is living out of the gospel; the other is living out of the "bad news" of your own making.

Check off the assignments you've completed:

☐ Listened to Message 3

☐ Memorized Romans 1:17

☐ Completed the exercises

☐ Read "The Weak, Strong, Right, and Wrong"

☐ Updated your prayer partner

Answer key to Question 2:

1: A, 2: B, 3: B, 4: A, 5: A, 6: A, 7: B

Session

4 LAW AND THE GOSPEL

We abuse law by turning it into our gospel, by making law our good news instead of what Christ has done for us. In doing so, we lose both the law and the gospel. At the heart of this abuse is a legalistic heart that says, "Give me a law so that I can keep it, and feel righteous about it."

GOALS:

- To understand the difference between living under the law and living under the gospel
- To see how prone we are to live under law—in subtle as well as obvious ways—and how that overflows into an unloving approach toward others
- To know in a greater way that Christ has set us free from bondage to the law and, through the gospel, empowers us to grow in fulfilling the law's intention

>>> LISTEN TO MESSAGE 4

MESSAGE OUTLINE

1. The problem is with us!

2. Mistaken expectations: capsizing the law (practical legalism)

    a. Telltale sign #1: Looking for credit for your good deeds

    b. Telltale sign #2: Defensiveness

    c.   Telltale sign #3: Comparing yourself with others

    d.   Telltale sign #4: Reputation fixation

3.   Misunderstood diagnosis: trivializing the law

    a.   Problem #1: We give the law a power it was never meant to have.

    b.   Problem #2: We have a suspect motive (power) for relying on the law to change us.

54 *Session 4*

   c.   Problem #3: We forget God's real target.

   d.   Problem #4: We underestimate the flesh (sinful nature).

4.   Misplaced dependency: idolizing the law

HOMEWORK

Name: Due:

Memorize:

We know that the law is good if one uses it properly.
—1 Timothy 1:8

Complete the following questions and exercises:

1. Read the summary below concerning the law:

Law is good because it:	Law is powerless because it cannot:
shows us how our faith should express itself	maintain our relationship with God and others
shows us what Jesus is like	give us righteousness
reveals the character of God	justify those who break it
brings sanity, wisdom, and direction	free us from bondage, guilt, and corruption
drives us to Christ and his Spirit	give us power
restrains wickedness	give us life
convicts of sin	provide us with a substitute
is written on our hearts	give us the gift of the Spirit
is part of love	cleanse our conscience

2. The Israelites had the finest system of law ever given, yet they all died in the desert, without ever reaching the promised land. What does this tell you about the power or capability of law?

What did the Israelites lack?

When I come to church on time, that's a good thing. However, when I use that fact to feel more righteous than someone else who's often late, I'm abusing the law to feel superior to that person. When I come on time so that people will think well of me, I'm perverting the law for the purpose of self-righteousness. When I resent those who come late, I'm perverting the law as the Pharisees did. The real law of God tells me to love my neighbor, and not resent him because of his so-called failures. Furthermore, there are times when even I break my own law, and arrive late. At that point, I feel less righteous, and so make excuses and defend myself.

3. Describe three laws that you tend to add onto the work of Christ, in order to create your own sense of righteousness. How do you feel when you've obeyed your laws—and others haven't? How do you feel when *you* fail to obey your own laws?

4. How does living this way affect your relationship with Jesus? Give examples.

Our hearts are a nonstop law-producing factory. According to our desires, fears, and hopes, we produce laws to try to accomplish what we desire. "Don't arrive late." "Why is this place such a mess?" "Don't talk back to me!" Of course, it's loving not to talk back or interrupt someone. The problem, however, is that we often bash people over the head with our laws and feel justified in doing so. In such cases, we use law to try to control, manipulate, and intimidate other people. Significantly, Paul did not speak in Romans 1:5 of the "obedience that comes from nagging"! Rather, he spoke about the "obedience that comes from faith." For Paul, the law has no power to produce the heart obedience God is looking for.

5. List three laws you've made for your spouse, children, or friends.

6. Have any of these laws ever been effective in changing that person?

7. How does your use of these laws make that person feel? (Note: Ask that person directly, but ask in an inviting manner, since he or she may be afraid to tell you! For example, "I've been thinking about how I come across. I've realized I can often seem quite harsh and intense. Can you tell me how you feel when I say . . . ?" Write down that person's answer.

8. Place a check by the three or four items you most see in yourself under each category below.

   By living by unbelief and under the law—

   ☐ I live as though my actions will make God or other people approve of me.

   ☐ I become preoccupied with myself.

   ☐ I foster an independent spirit.

   ☐ I become critical and judgmental.

   ☐ I develop a performance lifestyle for myself and others.

   ☐ I tend to be dominated by fears and anxieties.

   ☐ I require extra effort to complete a task—which reveals my unbelief.

   ☐ I develop barriers to loving others.

   ☐ I find it hard, if not impossible, to forgive.

   ☐ I become distant from the love of Christ, thus affecting my outreach to the lost.

   ☐ I destroy my confidence in Christ's ability to bridge the gap between God's holiness and people's sinfulness.

   ☐ I base my worth on the "success" of my efforts.

   ☐ I feed my self-righteousness, and have trouble seeing when I'm wrong.

   By living by faith and under grace—

   ☐ I run to the Father because I know he loves me. I receive his delight in me (Zephaniah 3:17) and respond by delighting in him.

   ☐ I believe that my sins are forgiven—enabling me, through the Spirit, to love and forgive others. I'm able to cultivate a lifestyle of forgiveness!

   ☐ I receive by faith my new position as a son/daughter, for whom there is now no condemnation.

   ☐ I understand the power of the sinful nature, the damage it can do, and the powerlessness of the law to control it.

   ☐ I know that only through the Spirit's power can I love my neighbor.

☐ I can break down barriers to loving others.

☐ I can experience peace and contentment as a dominant theme in my life.

☐ I can go to my heavenly Father in prayer with all my struggles, problems, and needs.

☐ I experience an ever-increasing desire, given by the Holy Spirit, to see God glorified in all I do, say, or think.

☐ My worth is determined by the gospel.

☐ I have become preoccupied with Jesus, and have a desire to see his will and kingdom purposes accomplished.

In Christ, I am free from the law's condemnation. In Christ, my sins are paid for, and I have Jesus' perfect obedience. Law does not determine my acceptance with God. Now I know law cannot sanctify me. It cannot make me more kind, gentle, and loving. I am also free from using law against others. Since I know law has no power to change my heart, I realize that this is true for other people as well.

9. Describe a situation where you've been living "under law." How could this situation be different as you live by faith and under grace? Be specific.

10. Describe a recent example of when you were more concerned about being *seen* as a sinner rather than *being* a sinner. How would living by faith and under grace change how you view your sin? Again, be specific.

In preparation for Session 5:

Teach someone else (a Christian or non-Christian) about the practical implications of justification by faith. Focus on the impact of received righteousness, and include a recent illustration or story from your own life in which you've struggled for righteousness. Be sure to include relevant passages from Scripture as you explain justification.

Once you're done teaching, ask this person to explain back to you one practical application of justification by faith—and in particular, of received righteousness. What did he or she actually "take away" from your teaching?

As soon as possible after completing this assignment, go to Session 5 and answer questions 1 through 8.

READ

The End of the Struggle
—Stanley Voke, *Personal Revival*, © 1964

> *Jesus, Thy blood and righteousness*
> *My beauty are, my glorious dress.*

A small boy came home one day from Sunday school and said, "Mum, we had a new hymn today. It said that Jesus knows all about our struggles." Then pensively he added, "You know, that isn't right. We don't struggle. Only snails struggle." This reminds me of a caption I once saw in a missionary magazine. It showed a snail crawling and a bird flying, under which were the words, "What are you—snail or bird?" Some African Christians, blessed at a convention, were seen going home singing, their faces shining with joy. Others said, "Look at those Christians—they are like birds flying." But they themselves knew how different it could be when their hearts were not right with Jesus. Then they could be like snails, earthbound, selfbound, struggling instead of soaring.

If we see only the plumbline putting us in the sinner's place so that we remain in the state of feeling sinful, we shall be like snails—struggling. Seeing sin does not set us free—we need to see Jesus. For every one look at sin, said Murray McCheyne, take ten looks at Christ. Then indeed we are like birds that fly.

The struggle for righteousness
J. B. Phillips translates the fourth verse of Romans 10 by saying, "Christ means the end of the struggle for righteousness," thus throwing light on the Authorized Version [KJV]: "Christ is the end of the law for righteousness. There is in all of us a struggle to get and keep our own righteousness, which is why it is so hard to come to the sinner's place.

This struggle is as old as Adam and Eve who, when charged with sin in Eden, at once put the blame on one another and finally on the serpent, while at the same time they made garments of fig leaves to give themselves some sort of covering from the holy eyes of God. By the time of the New Testament, the struggle was well under way, for the whole Jewish religion was a developed attempt to achieve righteousness by works. Of the Jews of his day, Paul said, they were ever "going about to establish their own righteousness," rather than submit themselves to the righteousness of God.

We are all the same. Have you ever watched children build a sand castle on the beach before an incoming tide? Frantically they heap up their walls, patting the soft sand into solidity and reinforcing it with sticks and stones only to see it washed away at the last. So we go round and round to establish our defenses against the waves of other people's criticisms. For some of us life becomes one long struggle to be what we know all too well we are not.

The struggle for attainment

One phase of this battle for our own righteousness is the struggle to reach a standard of perfection. We have seen how the plumbline of God holds us to a perfect standard and the danger is that life may become a prolonged attempt to reach it. We become Christians under law instead of grace, so that instead of living in peace, we are torn with tension. Sometimes we set the standard ourselves by picturing the kind of Christian we ought to be. We follow an ideal image in our minds. It is as though we see the man we ought to be standing on some lofty height calling us on as we struggle vainly up the slopes, yet he never lends us a helping hand.

Of course other people set the standard for us too. Everyone can tell us what we ought to be. We hear sermons and read books showing us the kind of Christians we should be, which only makes us feel guilty if we are sensitive, and self-satisfied if we are not. People put us on pedestals expecting this and that of us until life becomes one long struggle to be what others demand. So we live on under law trying to keep up to standards, while behind us is God's relentless law never letting us off; never lifting us up.

Are you a Christian living under law? Living under continual condemnation because you feel all the time you ought to be a better Christian, who prays more, does more, gives more? You are chained to a moral yardstick. You live under a yoke and a burden when all the while Jesus wants to give you rest.

The struggle to keep our reputation

Another aspect of this struggle for righteousness is the fight for reputation. We are all reputation-conscious. Some of us have a reputation—it may be for piety, efficiency, leadership, preaching, housekeeping, anything! Others of us wish we had a reputation. Once acquired, or assumed, it can haunt us, dog us, browbeat us, wear us to shreds. Bondage to reputation can be sheer slavery, and yet did we but know, it is only a form of struggle for our own righteousness. We are unwilling to be known as failures along any line.

The struggle for appearance

The struggle for righteousness consequently becomes the struggle for appearance, which simply means that somewhere we end up with being dishonest about ourselves. I once heard a man speak to children about eggs. He had three of them with labels attached. One egg was stale and it told us it was not what it used to be. The second was half-hatched and it announced it was not what it hoped to be. But the third was rotten and although it looked good, was honest enough to tell us it was not what it seemed to be.

Is it not true that we seem to be what we are not, like the Jews whose struggle for righteousness led them inevitably into hypocrisy. The trouble with success is that we dare not be failures, for if we are to keep our reputation we cannot admit ignorance or sin. That would be to collapse the sand castle before the tide had even come in. It is better to struggle on even to breaking point than admit some need that would mean others knowing us as we really are.

The tragedy of all this is the idea that we find favor with God by reaching standards. This is precisely where we are wrong. Again Phillips's translation helps us in Romans 10, verse 5: "The man who perfectly obeys the law shall find life in it"—which is theoretically right but impossible in practice. If we could attain God's standard we should be blessed. But we cannot, so we end by being cursed. The very law that was designed to give us life has become the means of death, not because there is anything wrong with the standard itself, but because we sinners are unable to reach it.

Christ, the end of the struggle

What a relief it is when we see Christ as the end of all this. He is the end of the struggle for righteousness since He not only fulfilled the law for us, but was cursed for us as well. He has not only attained our perfection but atoned for our imperfection. There is nothing more to struggle about, for He has done all for us and God asks nothing now but our repentance and faith.

> *All the fitness He requireth*
> *Is to feel your need of Him.*

How beautifully Joy Davidman puts it: "The only way to get rid of sin is to admit it, for without honesty, repentance, forgiveness and grace are impossible. The Christian does not go around all the time feeling guilty. For him sin is a burden he can lay down for he can admit it, repent and be forgiven. It is the unfortunate creature who denies the existence of sin in general and his own in particular who must go on carrying it. The way to freedom consists in honest confession and repentance that can open our hearts to the Comforter." To open our souls to God's grace means He not only saves us from being the people we are, but changes us into those we ought to be.

How easy it is! The only way to get rid of sin is to admit it! Why is this so hard? Surely because it means letting go our own righteousness which is the very thing we do not like doing. Yet how can we have Christ's perfect robe of righteousness if we insist on keeping our own? It is impossible.

Jesus is our perfect righteousness. When we come to Him we need no other. The struggle for righteousness is over and He becomes our reputation and glory. We need not fear to come to the sinner's place, for when we do, it is to cease from our own works, to stop trying to be what we are not and admit instead what we are. At that point we accept Christ's own righteousness, we are justified before God and enter into peace. This is God's basic blessing for us, and the only true way of peace and joy.

Cast your deadly doing down,
Down at Jesus' feet.
Stand in Him, in Him alone,
Gloriously complete.

Check off the assignments you've completed:

☐ Listened to Message 4

☐ Memorized 1 Timothy 1:8

☐ Completed the exercises

☐ Read "The End of the Struggle"

☐ Updated your prayer partner

Session

5 THE EMPOWERING SPIRIT

The speaker's great sin against her daughter was that she didn't reach her daughter's conscience. In fact, she didn't even try . She felt that if she worked on her daughter's outward behavior, it would work inward. But true life change never works that way. In the speaker's words, "I built the house without a door. I presented the gospel like law, and I was not broken before her."

GOALS:

- To know the powerful ministry of the Holy Spirit at work in our lives—assuring, reminding, comforting, and applying the gospel to our hearts
- To know that the Spirit convicts and leads us to Christ, transforming us into Christ's likeness and empowering us for service
- To understand how faith and prayer are central to our walking with the Spirit

>>> LISTEN TO MESSAGE 5

MESSAGE OUTLINE

1. The chief obstacle: the "I" problem

2. The chief helper: the Holy Spirit

3. The heart of the matter: cultivating the heart of a son/daughter

4. A new confidence: the end of the struggle

HOMEWORK

Name: Due:

Memorize:

> May the God of hope fill you with all joy and peace as you
> trust in him, so that you may overflow with hope by the
> power of the Holy Spirit.
>
> —*Romans 15:13*

Complete the following questions and exercises:

1. Reflect on your teaching assignment (see page 62), about the practical implications of justification by faith. Describe the personal illustration you used.

2. When you asked that person afterward to explain one practical application of justification by faith (and in particular, of received righteousness), what was the response? Write it below.

3. If you had the chance to do this exercise again, what would you do differently and why?

4. Overall, what impact do you think your discussion had? How much do you think the other person actually understood?

5. What would you like to change or develop further, in terms of your attitude and approach to sharing Christ with others?

6. Keeping your teaching experience in mind, look over the questions below. Do any in particular leap out at you? Using these questions as a guide, reflect once more on your teaching time.

- How did you respond to being assigned this task?
- Was there a flight or fear response?
- Was there a fight or teeth-grinding response?
- Did you find yourself responding like a slave—questioning the assignment, complaining, or feeling burdened with the task?
- Did you do the task dutifully, yet without passion, or with a sense of self-confidence or self-righteousness?
- Did you find yourself responding like an orphan—depending on your own resources and feeling alone, incompetent, helpless, guilty, or impotent?
- As you proceeded, was there a love for Christ and a desire to share him?
- Was there a love for the other person?
- To what extent did fear of failure and fear of rejection come into play?
- Did you seek the other person's approval?
- What was your praying like?
- Did the busyness of your world crowd out your praying?
- Did you complete the assignment without much expectation of God's power and glory being revealed?
- As you shared, did you have a sense of your Father's partnership and the Spirit's presence?
- Did you see evidence of the Spirit in the fruit of humility, peace, joy, gentleness, confidence, and courage?

Check the following box when you've completed your reflection. ☐

7. With your answers to the above questions in mind, what was the overall impact of this teaching assignment on you?

The speaker concluded that her real sin against her daughter was her attempt to control her outward behavior. She was not really able to connect with her daughter until the Holy Spirit brought her to a deeper conviction of sin into her own life. Only after she was broken herself, could her daughter begin to hear her. Most parents are willing to say, "I'm sorry I got angry." However, it is when our own hearts are truly broken before God, that our kids hear what we are saying. Kids need to know that Mom and Dad are the biggest sinners in the house who desperately need Jesus, just as they do. So we reach our children and others through our brokenness, weakness, and repentance—not through pounding the law into them.

8. Think of a family relationship where someone needs to hear the truth about you and the gospel—that you are a needy sinner. How might you apply what you're learning to this relationship?

9. The speaker discussed how the Holy Spirit taught her to pray—particularly against what the enemy was doing in her daughter's life. Where has your life been under attack by the enemy and his lies? Write down the lies you've been believing; and then, opposite each lie, write the truth of the gospel you should be believing.

10. Think of one person you care about, and what you believe the enemy has done in his or her life. Write those things below. Begin praying about your answers to questions 8 through 10, and inform your prayer partner about them.

READ
Dead Man Walking

In the movie *Dead Man Walking*, the lead character is on death row, and is brought from his cell down the hallway to the death chamber where he will be electrocuted. Thus, he is a "dead man walking."

This scene is also a picture of each one of us. We are all walking down the hallway to our death. We live on death row. All of us are "dead men walking." However, God's justice and our sin demand something far worse than the electric chair; we deserve the eternal wrath of God.

Amazingly, as we're taken down that hallway, we discover that we've been brought into a great courtroom instead of the death chamber. The jailer shuts the door behind us, we look up, and see a very impressive-looking judge sitting behind the bench.

"You know that you're on the way to the electric chair, don't you?" Each of us nods in acknowledgment.

"Well," he says, "I'm going to pardon you. Would you like to be pardoned for your many crimes, your sin? Would you like to be forgiven so that there's no more guilt, no more condemnation for your crimes?" Of course, each of us says, "Yes, Your Honor!"

At that moment, the lights in the courtroom flicker and become dim. The judge explains, "Someone who loves you more than you can dream or imagine has just been electrocuted in your place." He goes on, "Consider yourself pardoned by the power that has been bestowed on me. You are forgiven!"

Now this is the first part of justification by faith: pardon and forgiveness. But there is more. Think of some famous people who have been acquitted or pardoned by the court system. In our minds many of us still think of them as guilty. The pardon or "not guilty" verdict did not change our opinion of them.

So let's go back to the courtroom scene again. The judge looks at us and says, "I know that when you leave this courtroom, many people—even among your own family and friends—will still consider you guilty. So I'm not merely going to forgive you.

"I'm going to give you a gift, and that gift is a new reputation. This new reputation means that you are completely right. I am declaring that you have no blemish, no sin, and no guilt. So not only are you pardoned and completely forgiven, but now you are also completely righteous. You will leave this courtroom with this new reputation."

This is the second part of justification by faith: a new reputation—the declaration that we are righteous. We are not only declared "not guilty," but we also have a new reputation. Therefore, to live out of our justification is to go back constantly to that courtroom scene. Every day, we have to keep recognizing that we are pardoned, declared not guilty, and instead declared completely righteous.

We return to the courtroom one more time. There's one other thing the great judge says to us: "You have been pardoned and declared right. I'm going to let you go free. But you probably do not have a family to go to." So the judge takes off his robe and comes down from the bench. (He is dressed in jeans, T-shirt, and sneakers.) He puts his arm around us and says, "Would you like to come and live with me as my children? Would you like to be adopted? I have a room for you in my mansion. I will provide you everything you will ever need for life. You will have countless brothers and sisters there, who will love you and whom you will love. And I will make you an heir to everything that I own."

"How on earth is all this possible?" we ask. The Judge then explains, "I want you to understand that all of this is possible because of my one and only Son, Jesus. He lived a perfect life so that you could have his perfect record. He suffered terribly for you, and rose again for your justification. All of this, he did for you. And for this reason, once I adopt you, I will view you exactly as I do him—sinless and holy. Since you are adopted into my family, I am making you a co-heir with him. What's more, I am going to give you all the help you need to live in my family."

So this great Judge who has now become your Father provides you with another person, the Holy Spirit, to indwell you, to give you the power to live this new life. The Spirit is the one who will lead you "in the way everlasting." Your Father knows that you cannot possibly live this life on your own, so he gives you his Holy Spirit to indwell you, convict you of sin, comfort you, teach you, and reassure you of God's great love for you.

So, for example, as you become more and more secure in this truth about yourself you'll be able to listen to criticism—even unfair criticism—without having to prove that you're right. You'll be able to listen in order to see what you can learn; you can listen to see how you can help the other person who's criticizing you. You can actually be more concerned for him than you are for yourself. You no longer have to prove that you are right and okay, because your identity with God is right and secure.

Check off the assignments you've completed:

☐ Listened to Message 5

☐ Memorized Romans 15:13

☐ Completed the exercises

☐ Read "Dead Man Walking"

☐ Updated your prayer partner

6

FELLOWSHIP WITH THE FATHER

For us to live before God, we have to stop living before other people. George Mueller noted two things that had to happen in his life before he became effective in delighting in God and getting into the warfare of prayer. First, Mueller said, "I had to die to what George Mueller thinks about George Mueller. You really can't live for God's glory or have fellowship with God if you are thinking about what you think of yourself." Second, he added, "The day had to come when I had to die to what other people thought about me."

GOALS:

- To have greater fellowship, enjoyment, and partnership with our Father through prayer
- To have a greater appreciation for prayer as a powerful weapon of the gospel
- To understand what inhibits our prayer life

>>>> LISTEN TO MESSAGE 6

MESSAGE OUTLINE

1. The real issue: fellowship with your Father

2. John Owen: "A giant Christ leads to giant Christians."

3. Examples from the life of Samuel Johnson

4. The real question: Do you really enjoy God?

5. George Mueller: dying to your opinion of yourself

6. Preparing to meet with the Father each morning
   a. Realizing that God is ready to meet with you and reveal himself

    b.   Preparing to see your attitude changed

    c.   Preparing to "walk the law" (Matthew 7:12)

7.   Self-forgetful prayer

8. The heart (and cost) of ministry

HOMEWORK

Name: Due:

Memorize:

"The LORD your God is with you, he is mighty to save. He
will take great delight in you, he will quiet you with his love,
he will rejoice over you with singing."
                                        —*Zephaniah 3:17*

Complete the following questions and exercises:

1. Read the following list regarding positive attitudes toward prayer:

    *   God is really interested in my conversing with him.
    *   Prayer will accomplish much good; it is not pointless.
    *   God longs to capture my heart.
    *   I am as independent and self-willed as God says I am.
    *   I have a spirit of timidity that desperately needs God.
    *   Through prayer the Father will give me his Spirit.
    *   Prayer is worth the time. God is enjoyable.
    *   Prayer is a great investment of my time.

- I desperately need God, even when I am not in a crisis.
- The Father is there; he hears me, and he will respond.
- His response is always very good, even if my circumstances do not improve.
- I am involved in a spiritual battle.
- I pray not to change God, but for God to change me.
- People can be converted or changed through my prayers.
- Prayer is a time of adoration and personal worship.

2. What three items from the above list would you most like to be truer of your attitude toward prayer? Why?

Psalm 37:4 reads, "Delight yourself in the LORD, and he will give you the desires of your heart." Often we interpret this to mean that if only we will delight in the Lord we will get what we want, thus making our "delighting" a way of manipulating God. However, we need to remind ourselves that delighting in God can only occur as we receive, by faith, God's delight in us. The more we receive God's love and delight in us, the more we will delight in and desire him. As God becomes our chief desire, God's desires and ours start to become identical.

So focus on what God does for you. Think about the implications of this session's memory verse: God delighting in you and quieting you with his love. The Spirit has the power to infuse this truth into your heart so that it becomes more than words—so that it transforms your experience with your Father. It's not so much what you "achieve" in devotions, but what you receive. It is not so much "having devotions" but enjoying a daily relationship with the Father. Consider renaming "devotions" as "fellowship time" to highlight the fact that the primary purpose of your time is not to meet a goal or go through a routine, but to be with your Father.

3. Does the idea of spending time with your Father seem rather pointless, exciting, or something else? Explain your answer.

4. What is the difference between meeting with the Father and "having devotions"? What does that look like for you?

George Mueller noted that his partnership with the Father prospered through his increasing awareness that he had to die to what he thought of himself, and had to die to what others thought of him as well.

5.   Where might you have to die, in order for your fellowship with the Father to grow? Give two examples; they can either be views or opinions you have about yourself, or opinions that others have of you.

In James 4:1–4 we read, "What causes fights and quarrels among you? Don't they come from your desires that battle within you? You want something but don't get it. You kill and covet, but you cannot have what you want. You quarrel and fight. You do not have, because you do not ask God. When you ask, you do not receive, because you ask with wrong motives, that you may spend what you get on your pleasures. You adulterous people, don't you know that friendship with the world is hatred toward God? Anyone who chooses to be a friend of the world becomes an enemy of God."

And yet, Jesus says in Matthew 21:22, "If you believe, you will receive whatever you ask for in prayer." If we believe that we'll receive whatever we ask for in prayer, why doesn't it happen? Why don't we receive? James gives us the answer: We ask with the wrong motives. We ask so that we can spend what we get on our pleasures. This is much broader than money; it is speaking about satisfying our own desires. But isn't that how most of us pray?

And what kind of people are we, when we pray in that manner? James is clear: We are adulterous. What is an adulterer like? Adultery is a terrible word! It means, among other things, that we're seeking to use another person for our own pleasure. But in this case, it's *God* whom we're attempting to use. This is more than being manipulative. Adultery is also seductive in trying to get what we want from the other person. So we must keep in mind that our hearts are seductive. We try to manipulate and seduce God for our own pleasure. So we try and "delight" in him, so he'll give us what we want. And we will continue to "delight" in him—as long as our pleasures are being fulfilled. James ends with a warning that to live like this is to be a friend of the world.

6. When have you prayed for something—maybe even something good—but with wrong motives? How did God answer that prayer? What did you learn from that experience?

7. If you lost everything in this world—all your money, status, family—and had nothing left but your relationship with God, would you have all that you need? Explain.

8. Reflect again on your answer to question 7. How do you think your current perspective is affecting your relationship with God? Again, explain your answer.

Two great hindrances to genuine prayer are *legalism* and *license*. Legalism destroys genuine prayer, for it prays for the purpose of self-righteousness—to look good to God, others, and ourselves. It prays, "Thank you, Lord, that I am not like other people, who do not pray like I do, who do not live like I do." It prays without compassion and relationship. It prays long prayers for show, to create an impression. License also destroys genuine prayer, for it does not pray. It is lazy, unconcerned, and self-sufficient. License seeks self-gratification from things in this world; thus, it has no concern with things that are not of this world.

9. How have you seen your self-gratification and self-righteousness hinder genuine prayer? Give examples.

Often, we do not pray bold prayers. Rather we lapse into clichés that arise from our alienation from God and a lack of desire to be close to him. Frequently our prayers are "safe"; they focus on anything but our hearts, in an attempt to keep God at a distance. Many times, we're not honest with God about where we are, and give little thought to the implications of what we pray.

10. What would be a bold, daring, and risky prayer for you?

11. What are some of the implications of this risky prayer? In other words, in what ways will your heart have to change for this prayer to be answered?

12. Share your answers to questions 10 and 11 with your prayer partner, and begin to pray regarding these areas. Check the following box when you have done so. ☐

13. How has your understanding of "devotions" and prayer changed or developed because of this study?

READ

Self-Forgetful Prayer

It should be the desire of every Christian to become a "reproducing Christian"—that is, one who promotes faith in Jesus in others by his testimony and example. To do so is to fulfill the most fundamental calling given to us by Jesus in Matthew 28:19, "Go and make disciples of all nations." This is an awesome goal. It means nothing less than asking all people to give up their self-will and to return to utter dependence upon God—for salvation and from sin and its punishment (death), and for life and all things pertaining to life. It means being God-centered through Christ Jesus instead of self-centered.

Now this task, if understood properly, will inevitably create a tension in us as we try to carry it out—because, at root, we ourselves are still selfish and self-willed. We still nourish our own ambitions, our own expectations for ourselves and others, and our own desires. Worse, we still claim the right to harbor certain grudges against others. We hold on to hurt from others, which we have cultivated through years of careful attendance and devotion. In short, we are selfish. If we hope to speak effectively to others about giving up their self-will and becoming disciples of Jesus, we must first remove the planks of wood from our own eyes. We must become increasingly God-centered and increasingly self-forgetful, desiring his will and seeking his way of accomplishing that will.

How is this to be done? Prayer is the means chosen by God. Along with faith, it is the most effective weapon of spiritual warfare offered to us. By it, we lose our self-will and become God-centered. Prayer gives us power to do God's will in God's way. It enables us to identify with God's will, submit to it, and dare others to commit themselves to it. Through prayer, the kingdom of self is broken down and the kingdom of God lifted up.

How do we pray in such a way?

Obviously, if this is the case, teaching others to pray in a kingdom manner is critical to the healthy life of all Christians. The following steps outline two important elements in prayer.

Step 1: Pray as a son or daughter of the King (Galatians 4:4–7). It is critical to recognize, right at the beginning of prayer, that we are here for fellowship with God. We are his children, coming to communicate with our Father—to enjoy him, worship him, and adore him. We make a mistake when we rush off into other areas of prayer before acknowledging this foundational fact.

There will be times when this fellowship registers itself to us in an experiential way. You may feel or sense God's presence while bowing your heart to him, praising him, reviewing the way he called you to faith, giving thanks for the provisions he has made, and especially upon considering the cross of Christ and the access to God it has provided for you. "In him and through faith in him we may approach God with freedom and confidence" (Ephesians 3:12). On the other hand, there will be times when no sensation of God's presence is experienced. Don't fret over this, or struggle to feel something. Count on the truth of Scripture. When you cry out in the name of Jesus, you are in God's presence whether you feel it or not. Jesus says in John 14:23, "If anyone loves me, he will obey my teaching. My Father will love him, and we will come to him and make our home with him."

No matter what we do or don't feel, it's our privilege to come before the King of kings and Lord of lords—to enjoy communion with our Father in heaven who has blessed us in the heavenly realms with every spiritual blessing in Christ Jesus, who has chosen us before the creation of the world, predestined us to be adopted as his sons, redeemed us, and revealed great things to us (Ephesians 1:3–8). Enjoy him!

Step 2: Pray throughout the day against those things which hinder our fellowship with God. That involves confessing to God our sins, all of which hinder our fellowship with him. There are many sins that hinder our fellowship. One major sin, for example, is anxiety (Romans 8:15). It is major, because it reveals self-centeredness. It makes plain that the kingdom of self is raging and reigning. Anxiety reveals that we have ambitions, devotions, desires, dreams, demands, and expectations. It shows a decided lack of faith in God's ability to provide. It is focused on self instead of God.

The best way to eliminate anxiety and its stumbling block to fellowship is to determine whether our ambitions are the Lord's, and then pray for the kingdom's success. That is God-centeredness, making us partners with God. Our worries then become his worries, too. If we're concerned about his concerns and not our own, we can let him "worry" about how they will finally be accomplished. "Not my will be done, but yours," is the heart of the prayer taught by Jesus to his disciples. It's worth noting that when Jesus faced the most anxious moments of his life, as he shrank from the prospect of a cruel death by crucifixion, he prayed that prayer. Though he went into prayer with beads of sweat because of the terror of the moment, he came away from it with power. He had committed himself to his Father's keeping. He had set aside his desire (life) and the anxiety that desire cultivated in the face of present difficulty, and taken up his Father's will (death on a cross in order to atone for our sins). Through prayer, he stood the test.

It is wonderful to realize that the concern of Jesus, which tempted him to such anxiety, was ultimately resolved for him by his Father—in the Father's time and in his own way. Jesus was raised from the grave in triumph—raised in an incorruptible body to die no more, but to live a full life forever. When our hearts are "fixed on things unseen," anxiety will be done away with, and this awful stumbling block to fellowship and effectiveness will be removed.

Check off the assignments you've completed:

☐ Listened to Message 6

☐ Memorized Zephaniah 3:17

☐ Completed the exercises

☐ Read "Self-Forgetful Prayer"

☐ Updated your prayer partner

Session

7 LIFESTYLE REPENTANCE

Repentance is *not* about figuring it all out, understanding your sin, and being able to use a methodology to speak eloquently great volumes about the nature of your sin without doing anything. As John Calvin noted, "It is easy to use the words faith and repentance, but they are the things that are most difficult to perform. The person, therefore, that makes the worship of God consist in these, by no means loosens the reins of discipline, but compels people to the course which they are most afraid to take."

GOALS:

- To understand the powerlessness of false repentance, and the joy and power of true repentance
- To see how the gospel motivates genuine repentance
- To remind us that God calls us to live a lifestyle of repentance

>>> LISTEN TO MESSAGE 7

MESSAGE OUTLINE

1. The life of faith and repentance

    a. Acts of contrition—not "God, I'll do better," but God at work within us

    b. Faith and repentance intertwined

    c. The difficulty of faith and repentance—John Calvin and Martin Luther

2. Mistaken ideas about repentance

    a. Confusion between repentance and its fruits—repentance is primarily relational

b. Not simply talking about change

c. Not a life of misery and groveling

3. A closer look

   a. Hosea 6, and Thomas Watson's six categories of repentance

   b. The obedience of faith vs. obedience to law (Romans 1:5)

   c. Hosea 14

HOMEWORK

Name: Due:

Memorize:

> This is what the Sovereign LORD, the Holy One of Israel,
> says: "In repentance and rest is your salvation, in quietness
> and trust is your strength, but you would have none of it."
> —*Isaiah 30:15*

Complete the following questions and exercises:

1. Review the diagram "The Heart God Revives" found at the end of this lesson.

2. In the diagram, check three items under the "Proud People" column that you have most seen in yourself. Below, write down a recent example of each.

3. Ask your prayer partner to pray about the three characteristics you chose in question 2. Check the following box when you have done this. ☐

4. Write a brief definition of repentance below:

There is a crucial difference between what we normally call repentance and what Scripture says is real repentance. Hosea 7:13b–14a reads, "I long to redeem them but they speak lies against me. They do not cry out to me from their hearts but wail upon their beds." This passage draws a distinction between "crying out" and "wailing."

5. What do you think is the difference between crying out and wailing, and why is God so concerned about this distinction?

Another important passage concerning this topic is Hosea 6:1–4: "'Come, let us return to the LORD. He has torn us to pieces but he will heal us; he has injured us but he will bind up our wounds. After two days he will revive us; on the third day he will restore us, that we may live in his presence. Let us acknowledge the LORD; let us press on to acknowledge him. As surely as the sun rises, he will appear; he will come to us like the winter rains, like the spring rains that water the earth.' 'What can I do with you, Ephraim? What can I do with you, Judah? Your love is like the morning mist, like the early dew that disappears.'"

What is wrong with this picture? It looks as though Israel is repentant, because they are talking about returning to the Lord (Hosea 6:1). They acknowledge God. They know that he is able to heal them so that they can live in his presence. They say that they know God will come to them. It sounds pretty good! It sounds as though they are full of faith. Nevertheless, this is an example of false repentance. The NIV titles this section "Israel Unrepentant." We clearly see that there is a problem when God answers them in verse 4. God is displeased with their words. He knows their love is like the morning mist that soon disappears. Israel is unrepentant, and their "returning" is a form of pain relief. They want the pain and suffering removed, and they want it done quickly—in two or three days.

Sadly, this is not very different from how most of us repent. Say, for instance, I've said something to my wife that's hurt her. How will I typically deal with it? I might say, "I'm sorry I hurt you. I shouldn't have said that. Will you forgive me?" Very likely, she'd respond with something like, "You know, that really did hurt, and right now I'm not sure that forgiveness is the issue." And I would say (or at least think to myself), "I *said* I'm sorry. If you can't forgive me, *you* have the problem."

At this point, my wife is feeling the impact of the deeper sin I've committed against her—the one I'm *not* repenting of. I've apologized for my words, but I haven't repented of the resentment, anger, and hatred in my heart—all of which she has felt. The truth is that I am still unrepentant, since what I'm after is quick reconciliation and relief from the pain. Furthermore, if my wife points this out to me and I get angry, it's clear that I haven't repented.

6.   Describe a recent "repentance" that was just a form of pain relief—
     an attempt to "get it over with" as quickly as possible.

Matthew 27:3–5 describes Judas's "repentance." Judas was seized with
remorse over what he had done. He returned the money and so made
restitution. He also acknowledged that he had sinned and that he had
betrayed an innocent man. Clearly, Judas was very sorry for what he
had done. He even acted on his sorrow, and returning the large amount
of money he had gained. Yet, was Judas truly repentant?

Note that the important point is not whether Judas was sorry, but what
kind of sorrow it was. Many times, when we say "I'm sorry" we genuinely do feel remorse. Nevertheless, the essential issue is not how sorry
we are, or how bad we feel, but what kind of sorrow we have and what
comes out of that sorrow. "Godly sorrow brings repentance that leads
to salvation and leaves no regret, but worldly sorrow brings death"
(2 Corinthians 7:10).

7. What is your understanding of the difference between godly sorrow and worldly sorrow?

We agree that Judas was sorry. He made restitution, acknowledged his sin, and even specifically named his sin, yet hardly anyone would argue that this was genuine repentance. But isn't this how most of us repent? We say we're sorry, but there's something missing. Like Judas, we're often sorry for the consequences of our sin, but we fail to see or acknowledge the underlying sin of our hearts. We gloss over the fact that our hearts are rebellious, hateful, arrogant, controlling, stubborn, and idolatrous.

8. What do you think genuine repentance would have looked like for Judas?

9. What's necessary for you to cultivate a lifestyle of repentance, rather than simply "spot repent" and move on? What would need to happen? Be specific.

10. Check off one of the counterfeits below which you have confused with genuine repentance, and then give a recent example of that counterfeit from your life.

    ☐ changing your   ☐ making promises
        outward behavior   or resolutions

    ☐ groveling   ☐ engaging in self-pity

    ☐ beating yourself up   ☐ offering a sacrifice

    ☐ having a brilliant observation
        or insight about yourself or your sins

11. Conversely, talk about a time of brokenness and repentance in your life. How did the Spirit change you through that experience?

12. How would developing a lifestyle of genuine repentance lead to even deeper joy and spiritual power? What might that look like for you?

READ

I Can't Believe I Did That!

A lifestyle of repentance is not something we normally practice or think about. Rather than a lifestyle of repentance, most of us live a lifestyle of remorse and resolution. Our usual approach to our sin may be summarized as follows:

- **Remorse:** "I can't believe I did that!" "I just can't forgive myself."
- **Resolution:** "I promise to do better next time!" "I won't do *that* again."

Behind this way of living are two great misunderstandings about our hearts. First, we think too highly of ourselves. We loathe looking at our hearts and seeing what they're really like. Thus, we're constantly surprised at how angry, lustful, and hateful we can quickly become. Our response to our sin is then something along the lines of, "I can't believe I just did that." Bottom line: We don't believe what God says about our heart condition.

Second, we think we have the power to change our hearts. So in response to our sin, we make resolutions, or try to impose various laws on ourselves. Since we have a light view of our sin, we think that the law has power to change us. After all, if we have only a minor problem, a few resolutions and laws ought to be able to sort everything out.

Furthermore, since we usually approach our own sins in this way, we also approach the sins of others in a wrong manner. This can be summarized as follows:

- **Resent:** "I hate it when you do that!" "I wouldn't have done that."
- **React:** Angry thoughts, dirty looks, cutting words

Although we're often lenient with our own sins, we can be extremely harsh when it comes to the sins of others. We respond to our own sins with resolutions; we respond to the sins of others with resentment. As with our own sin, we're surprised at the sins of others, and our usual solution is to give them a couple of laws and send them on their way.

Given the state of our hearts, we shouldn't be surprised that we're called to live a lifestyle of repentance. Richard Lovelace notes that sin is "an

LIFESTYLE REPENTANCE

organic network of compulsive attitudes, beliefs and behavior deeply rooted in our alienation from God." Our hearts are an underground network of caves, all interconnected, and all full of sin. As light shines in, it reveals a cave together with passageways to ten more. Travel into another cave, and we find ten more passageways. This being the case, we shouldn't be surprised that we sin daily, and therefore need to repent daily.

Instead of the above responses, our usual response to our sin should be along the lines of:

- **Realize:** "I *did* do that." "I *can* believe that I am like that!"
- **Repent:** "Lord, forgive me! You're my only hope."

What does this genuine repentance look like? Hosea 14:1–9 describes this real repentance. In contrast to chapters 6 and 7, where Israel was demanding that the pain and agony cease, Hosea 14 describes people focusing on their sin. Their attitude is, "I did it." Remember that Hosea 6 describes us when we give a shallow confession, glossing over our heart sins, and then demanding quick forgiveness so we can go watch a movie. Meanwhile, the person we've sinned against feels lacerated and blown away by our contempt. Genuine repentance focuses on our sin and what's driving our hearts. It doesn't jump on the other person, demanding quick forgiveness.

In Hosea 14, the people finally concentrate on their sin. They acknowledge that their sin has been their downfall. Hosea 14:2 sums up gospel living. "Take words with you" means to be specific about our sin, including our heart sins. This verse teaches us to come to God, asking him to forgive our sins and receive us, so that we may worship him. Significantly, God's response in chapter 14 is very different from his response in Hosea 6:4. God now promises to heal and love his people.

Through repentance, God changes and renews us. Repentance is foundational to our lives, for through it we are healed and loved by God. Furthermore, from this repentance will flow a genuine love for people, and a realization that others are just like us—sinners who need the life-giving Holy Spirit.

Session 7 105

DIAGRAM: THE HEART GOD REVIVES

"The sacrifices of God are a broken spirit;
A broken and contrite heart, O God, you will not despise."

—Psalm 51:17

Proud People . . .	Broken People . . .
» focus on the failures of others.	» are overwhelmed with a sense of their own spiritual need.
» have a critical, fault-finding spirit; look at every one else's faults with a microscope, but their own with a telescope.	» are compassionate; can forgive much because they know how much they have been forgiven.
» are self-righteous; look down on others.	» esteem all others better than themselves.
» have an independent, self-sufficient spirit.	» have a dependent spirit; recognize their need for others.
» have to prove that they are right.	» are willing to yield the fight to be right.
» claim rights; have a demanding spirit.	» yield their rights; have a meek spirit.
» are self-protective of their time, their rights, and their reputation.	» are self-denying.
» desire to be served.	» are motivated to serve others
» desire to be a success.	» are motivated to be faithful and to make others a success.
» desire self-advancement.	» desire to promote others.
» have a drive to be recognized and appreciated.	» have a sense of their own unworthiness; are thrilled that God would use them at all.
» are wounded when others are promoted and they are overlooked.	» are eager for others to get the credit and rejoice when others are lifted up.
» have a subconscious feeling, "This ministry/church is privileged to have me and my gifts"; think of what they can do for God.	» have a heart attitude that says, "I don't deserve to have a part in any ministry"; know that they have nothing to offer God except the life of Jesus flowing through their broken lives.
» feel confident in how much they know.	» are humbled by how very much they have to learn.
» are self-conscious.	» are not concerned with self at all.

CONTINUED ››

Proud People . . .	Broken People . . .
» keep others at arm's length.	» are willing to risk getting close to others and to take risks of loving intimately.
» are quick to blame others.	» accept personal responsibility and can see where they are wrong in a situation.
» are unapproachable and defensive when criticized.	» receive criticism with a humble, open spirit.
» are concerned with being respectable, with what others think; work to protect their own image and reputation	» are concerned with being real; what matters to them is not what others think but what God knows; are willing to die to their own reputation.
» find it difficult to share their spiritual needs with others.	» are willing to be open and transparent with others as God directs.
» want to be sure that no one finds out when they have sinned; their instinct is to cover up.	» once broken, don't care who knows or who finds out; are willing to be exposed because they have nothing to lose.
» have a hard time saying "I was wrong; will you please forgive me?"	» are quick to admit failure and to seek forgiveness when necessary.
» tend to deal in generalities when confessing sin.	» are able to acknowledge specifics when confessing their sin.
» are concerned about the consequences of their sin.	» are grieved over the cause, the root of their sin.
» are remorseful over their sin, sorry they got found out or caught.	» are truly, genuinely repentant over their sin, evidenced by the fact that they forsake that sin.
» wait for the other to come and ask forgiveness when there is a misunderstanding or conflict in a relationship.	» take the initiative to be reconciled when there is a misunderstanding or conflict in relationships; they race to the cross; they see that if they can get there first, no matter how wrong the other may have been.
» compare themselves with others and feel worthy of honor.	» compare themselves to the holiness of God and feel a desperate need for His mercy.
» are blind to their true heart condition.	» walk in the light.
» don't think they have anything to repent of.	» realize they have need of a continual heart attitude of repentance.
» don't think they need revival, but are sure that everyone else does.	» continually sense their need for a fresh encounter with God and for a fresh filling of His Holy Spirit

Adapted from a message by Nancy Leigh DeMoss

© Life Action Ministries, P.O. Box 31, Buchanan, MI 49107-0031

SONSHIP

Check off the assignments you've completed:

☐ Listened to Message 7

☐ Memorized Isaiah 30:15

☐ Completed the exercises

☐ Read "I Can't Believe I Did That!"

☐ Updated your prayer partner

FAITH WORKING THROUGH LOVE

Those who are forgiven little, love little. Those who are forgiven much, love much. As your faith grabs hold of the finished work of Christ, and as he forgives you for your sins which are many, the Holy Spirit will work in your life to create something new. Ongoing faith is the instrument for receiving the power of the Spirit into your life, and for producing the fruit of love in your life.

GOALS:

- To understand that love is empowered by faith and the Spirit
- To recognize how easily we drift toward relying on our own sufficiency and righteousness
- To examine some practical applications of Galatians 5:6

>>> LISTEN TO MESSAGE 8

MESSAGE OUTLINE

1. What does God want you to do today?

2. What must we do to do the work of God (John 6:29)?

3. Receiving from God (active passivity)

4. The expression of faith (Galatians 5:6)

5. "Adding to the finished work of Christ"

6. The two faces of the flesh

7. Living by the Spirit

   a. The problem

   b. Responses of the flesh

   c. The response of faith

8. Lessons from Luke 7

   a. Love with the whole heart

b. Those forgiven much, love much

c. Simon's self-righteousness kept him from seeing his own sin

HOMEWORK

Name: Due:

Memorize:

For in Christ Jesus neither circumcision nor uncircumcision has any value. The only thing that counts is faith
expressing itself through love.

—*Galatians 5:6*

Go over the following section carefully before moving on to the exercises

Two ways of life

1. The circumcision mentality

People who follow this way of life are striving, through unbelief and the
wrong use of law, to become holy and to compel others to be holy. In
Paul's day "circumcision" was the outward act that represented an entire
system, a religion, which sought to obtain righteousness through the

law. It is a life of pretense; success is gauged by how many "converts" its followers can get to conform to this way of living, so that they can boast. Other people feel forced and compelled, and that they're accepted only when they conform to a set of laws.

2. The uncircumcision mentality
Followers of this way of life are striving, through unbelief and neglect of the law, to become happy. The uncircumcision lifestyle is not concerned about appearing good; rather, it stresses indulgence. "Eat, drink, and be merry, for tomorrow we die." In other words, circumcision is the legalistic way of living; uncircumcision is the licentious way of living.

Both ways of living are unloving to others, and both enslave those who practice them. Neither have any value whatsoever. We understand that the gospel has saved us from our disobedience, or uncircumcision mentality; we struggle to understand that the gospel also saves us from our "obedience," or circumcision mentality. The gospel saves us from our righteousness as well as our unrighteousness. Since both wrong approaches involve a life of bondage, they keep us from being free to love other people. Thus, the teaching in Galatians 5:6 may be paraphrased as follows: neither legalism nor licentiousness has any value. The only thing that counts is belief in the gospel, and loving others out of that belief. The only thing that should matter in our lives is our faith in Christ that expresses itself in love.

The following story gives a concrete example of how to apply Galatians 5:6:

> I have "map-reading righteousness." I know how to use maps; I never take a wrong turn, and I feel pretty good about it. My wife, on the other hand . . .
> One day in the car, she was reading a map and directing me where to drive. At one intersection, she told me to turn left. After I had turned left and driven about a mile, she suddenly said, "Oops, I'm sorry—we should have made a right turn back there."
> What was my response? Was it, "No problem, honey; I'll just turn around and go back"? No way! I responded with

FAITH WORKING THROUGH LOVE

something like, "Aahhgg—come on!" My face and expression oozed disapproval and contempt. After all, *I* wouldn't have made the same mistake. I'm always right when it comes to reading maps, so I have a right to explode.

Applying Galatians 5:6 to this incident would look something like this:

a. For in Christ Jesus neither circumcision
Correct map reading. This is a legalistic way of living, in which I get life from reading maps correctly, and condemning my wife for misreading them.

b. nor uncircumcision has any value
This would be flipping over to the opposite mentality. "Okay, if you don't like me being 'worried' about maps, then I don't care if we're lost forever, or arrive two hours late. I'm going to enjoy not caring." (Note: It's important to be aware of this opposite side, since we easily flip to licentiousness when our legalism doesn't work, and vice versa.)

c. The only thing that counts is faith
Map-reading has become my source of righteousness, my "good news," which basically means bad news for everyone else. Through the gospel, I see that I've misread God, and by choice. The gospel gives me all the righteousness I need. I don't need to be digging for it elsewhere. I go to the cross and repent of my hatred. I turn and rush into the loving arms of Jesus. I am overwhelmed by his mercy and love. I now see that my wife's misreading is not even by choice; it was merely a mistake. I now want to love her.

d. expressing itself through love
Believing the gospel frees me from the idol of control and self-righteousness in my life, I can respond lovingly: "It doesn't matter. We'll just turn around." In addition, in my heart I'll stop believing that I'm a perfect map-reader. I'm going to misread maps at some stage, and I now want to treat my wife the way I would like to be treated.

Complete the following questions and exercises:

1. Choose an area or example of "circumcision" in your own life—an area of legalism from which you draw righteousness. Think of an example when this mentality has manifested itself, and complete the following based on Galatians 5:6.

   a. *For in Christ Jesus neither circumcision*
      Describe the problem. How do you get rightness from this way of living?

   b. *nor uncircumcision has any value*
      What's the opposite of the above response? For example, if you chose "refrain from TV and computer games," the opposite would be an "entertainment junkie" who spends all day watching TV and playing games.

   c. *The only thing that counts is faith*
      What void are you trying to fill through this law, that you instead need to receive from the gospel through faith—for example, acceptance, love, power, joy, peace? Explain your answer.

d. *expressing itself through love*
    What would genuine love look like in your situation? How should that faith express itself? Describe the behavior that would naturally follow.

2. Now, choose an area or example of "uncircumcision" in your own life—an area of licentiousness which you enjoy and think will make you happy. It might even involve something you don't even have yet, but you think you'd be happy if you had it. Then again, complete the following based on Galatians 5:6:

a. *For in Christ Jesus neither uncircumcision*
    Describe the problem. Why do you think this behavior or thing makes (or would make) you happy?

b. *nor circumcision has any value*
    Again, describe the opposite response. For example, if you chose "plenty of good food, sweets, and snacks" as your example, the opposite would be a "health-Pharisee" who prides herself on eating correctly and properly, and judges those who outwardly love food.

c. *The only thing that counts is faith*
   Once more, what do you need to receive from the gospel
   through faith? Again, explain your answer.

d. *expressing itself through love*
   What would genuine love look like instead in your example? How would your faith express itself? Describe that
   behavior.

3. Reflect once more on your two examples from questions 1 and 2,
   and their opposites. What patterns of behavior jump out at you,
   from either direction? Where has your lack of faith become more
   apparent to you? Write your insights below.

Caught on tape!

Imagine for a moment that you're watching a reality TV show which features the life of an ordinary family—a husband and wife and their two children. Tonight's episode is set in the living room, and records how the husband interacts with his family. As you watch the show, you write down some statements made by the husband after certain incidents:

- His young daughter spills a drink on the sofa. As she tries to apologize, he says sharply, "Sorry isn't good enough. I told you to be careful!"
- Noticing some things lying around, he turns to his wife: "Boy, this place is a mess."
- His wife asks him to do something (while he is "busy" doing his own thing). He hears an irritated tone in her voice, and says, "What's your problem?"
- The two kids get into a fight and raise their voices. He shouts, "Stop making all that noise! Both of you, go to your rooms!"

4. Reflect on the above story, and answer the questions that follow:

   a. Describe what this husband is like.

   b. What does this husband need to repent of?

c. What areas or aspects of the gospel does he need to receive by faith into his heart?

d. How might you be like this husband? Describe a specific incident.

e. Based on the incident you just shared, what areas or aspects of the gospel do *you* need to receive by faith into *your* heart?

READ

What Is Faith?

—J. Gresham Machen, *What Is Faith?* Eerdmans, pages 216–18

When we come to see that what Paul calls the flesh is a mighty power, which is dragging us resistlessly down into an abyss of evil that has no bottom, then we feel our guilt and misery, then we look about for something stronger to help us than our own weak will.

Such a power is found by the Apostle Paul in faith; it is faith, he says, that produces or works itself out in, the life of love. But what does Paul mean when he says that "faith works"? Certainly he does not mean what the modern pragmatist skeptic means when he uses the same words; certainly he does not mean that it is merely faith, considered as a psychological phenomenon, and independent of the truth or falsehood of its object, that does the work. What he does mean is made abundantly clear in the last section of this same Epistle to the Galatians, where the life of love is presented in some detail. In that section nothing whatever is said about faith; it is not faith that is there represented as producing the life of love but the Spirit of God; the Spirit is there represented as doing exactly what, in the phrase "faith working through love," is ascribed to faith. The apparent contradiction leads us on to the right conception of faith. True faith, strictly speaking, does not do anything; it does not give, but receives. So when one says that we do something by faith that is just another way of saying that we do nothing—at least that we do nothing of ourselves. It is of the very nature of faith, strictly speaking, to do nothing. So when it is said that faith works through love, that means that through faith, instead of doing something for ourselves we allow someone else to help us. That force which enters our life at the beginning through faith, before we could do anything at all to please God, and which then strengthens and supports us in the battle that it has enabled us to begin, is the power of the Spirit of God.

The Christian preacher, then, comes before the world with a great alternative. Shall we continue to depend upon our own efforts, or shall we receive by faith the power of God? Shall we content ourselves with the materials which this world affords, seeking by endlessly new combinations to produce a building that shall endure; or shall we build with the materials that have no flaw? Shall we give men new motives, or ask God to give them a new power? Shall we improve the world, or pray God to create a new world? The former alternatives have been tried and found wanting: the best of architects can produce no enduring building when all the materials are faulty; good motives are powerless when the heart is evil. Struggle as we may, we remain just a part of this evil world until, by faith, we cry: "Not by might, nor by power, but by Thy Spirit, O Lord of Hosts."

Check off the assignments you've completed:

☐ Listened to Message 8

☐ Memorized Galatians 5:6

☐ Completed the exercises

☐ Read "What Is Faith?"

☐ Updated your prayer partner

9

SANCTIFICATION BY FAITH

It's critical to understand what the gospel is about—the depth of the love of God for us, the depth of our need, the lengths to which Jesus has gone, and the patience he has with us. When we begin to live out this gospel instead of trying to produce our own righteousness, love begins to work in our lives. Not that we do it perfectly, but through Christ's love we see the beginnings of real change.

GOALS:

- To know what genuine holiness looks like
- To understand how we change and grow in the Christian life

>>> LISTEN TO MESSAGE 9

MESSAGE OUTLINE

1. What does holiness look like? How do we become holy?

    a. Principle 1: The Christian life flows from the inside out (Matthew 23:25–26).

    b. Principle 2: I must be the first to change (Matthew 7).

2. How do we change? By believing the gospel (Galatians 3:3–5)!

3. What does this "change by believing" look like?
   a. One example: The family is late to church

   b. How I responded and why

   c. What I needed to start believing

    d.   Our hearts must change—duty is not enough

4.   What sin "feels" like

5.   What faith "feels" like

HOMEWORK

Name: Due:

Memorize:

> Are you so foolish? After beginning with the Spirit, are you
> now trying to attain your goal by human effort? Have you
> suffered so much for nothing—if it really was for nothing?
> Does God give you his Spirit and work miracles among you
> because you observe the law, or because you believe what
> you heard?
>
> *—Galatians 3:3–5*

Complete the following questions and exercises:

1. Which of the following phrases describe justification and which
    describe sanctification? Place a check mark under the "J" or the "S"
    indicating your choice.

	J	S	Justification or Sanctification?
a.	☐	☐	A growing love from a growing faith
b.	☐	☐	By faith apart from works
c.	☐	☐	Progressively being changed to resemble Christ
d.	☐	☐	Being declared legally righteous
e.	☐	☐	God's acquittal and acceptance of an enemy
f.	☐	☐	Continual inner cleansing and purification
g.	☐	☐	Once and for all at conversion
h.	☐	☐	Ongoing growth; never complete in this life
i.	☐	☐	The maturing of a son or daughter

2. Check your answers with the key at the end of this section. Check
    the following box when you have done this. ☐

3. Off the top of your head, write a definition of sanctification.

When we think about sanctification, we need to keep a number of things in mind. First and foremost, it is God who sanctifies us. The Holy Spirit alone has the amazing power to transform our hearts, conquer our idols, and cause us to delight in Jesus. We are not, however, passive in this process. We're called to live by repentance and faith, humbly believing and receiving the good news. Daily we are to live out of the gospel and love others. Every day we need to appropriate the righteousness and forgiveness that is ours through Christ. Each day we are to live out of God's delight in us. As we live by repentance and faith, we'll have a decreasing confidence in ourselves, and an increasing confidence in the Holy Spirit to transform our lives. As we grow, we become more aware of the sinful capabilities and expressions of our hearts, while also becoming more aware of the great capability of the Spirit to help us.

4. In a few paragraphs, describe how sanctification occurs in your life. In other words, how do you become more holy? How do you change? Include a specific personal example as an illustration.

5. Look over your answers to questions 3 and 4. Did you use biblical or theological language that is correct but has no real meaning for you? Did you use any clichés that are essentially irrelevant? Circle any such language, and rewrite these sections.

6. What are some incorrect, but commonly held, instinctive beliefs about how change takes place in our lives? (For one example, see Galatians 3:1–5.)

7. How can the principle of "faith working through love" encourage us, as we deal with people who are hard to love?

What is an idol? An idol is anything we believe we need apart from Jesus to make us happy, satisfied, or fulfilled. An idol arises when we desire something more than we desire Jesus; when we fear things other than God; when we worship ourselves rather than Christ; when we put our trust in anything other than God; when we serve any other thing rather than Jesus.

The reason we resort to idolatry isn't hard to find. When we fall away from God, we experience great need, deficiency, and alienation. In order to fulfill our lives we resort to idolatry. We serve, love, desire, trust, fear, and worship other things apart from God to give us love, joy, peace, freedom, status, reputation, identity, control, happiness, security, fulfillment, health, pleasure, significance, acceptance, and respect. Sometimes our idols are obviously wrong. However, many things we desire are often good in themselves—well-behaving children, for example. But even good things become idols when they start to rule our lives.

8. The speaker referred to his reputation, to "building a record," and to "serving so that he would be liked," as idols that were running his heart. Describe two idols that run your heart, and give a recent example of each.

9. What do these two idols promise you?

10. How do these idols eventually fail you? Be specific.

11. How do these two idols undermine your desire and ability to love?

12. Applying what you know about sanctification, how could the gospel impact these idols? What do you need to receive by faith from the gospel?

Faith involves giving up my own rightness for the righteousness of Christ. That is one reason why faith is so hard—it involves a continual dying to self. It is far easier to find my righteousness somewhere else (even in so-called "good deeds"), than to have to deal with the evil in my heart. It is that evil that propels me to find another easier path of least resistance, a false source of righteousness. It is far easier to keep a rule I have made up, or do a "good deed," than to daily face the ugly truth about my heart and my desperate need for Jesus.

13. The speaker referred to the change in his relationship with his wife when he began to relate by faith instead of unbelief. He noted that the first steps of faith feel like death. Why do you think living by faith feels like death? (Hint: How would you feel if you gave up the two idols you have described?)

In preparation for Session 10:

Teach someone else (a Christian or non-Christian) about the practical implications of sanctification by faith. In other words, explain to someone else how Jesus changes you, how the good news of Christ is transforming your relationships, and how "sanctification by repentance and faith" has impacted you and the struggles you face. Include a recent illustration or story from your own life, and think of creative ways to draw the person into what you're saying. For ideas, refer back to your answers earlier in this session, and read "The Power to Transform Us" at the beginning of Session 10.

Once you're done teaching, ask this person to explain back to you one practical application of sanctification by faith. What did he or she get out of your teaching?

As soon as possible after completing this assignment, go to Session 10 and answer questions 1 through 4.

Answer key to Question 1:

a: S, b: J, c: S, d: J, e: J, f: S, g: J, h: S, i: S

READ
Sanctification
— Richard Lovelace, *Dynamics of Spiritual Life*, pages 102–4

On several occasions the New Testament makes clear that cheap grace, the attempt to be justified through faith in Christ without commitment to sanctification, is illegitimate and impossible. The thrust of these passages is not really that we should add works to our faith, as if it were possible to advance one step forward into faith, but to hesitate before adding a second step into holiness. Faith and repentance are not separable quantities. To have faith is to receive God's Word as truth and rest upon it in dependent trust; to repent is to have a new mind toward God, one's self, Christ and the world, committing one's heart to new obedience to God. Obviously these two factors are so interwoven that they are experienced as one, so that the condition of justification is not faith plus repentance, but repentant faith. In the famous antiphony to Paul's teaching in James, it is clear that works and merit are not being added to the means of justification, but that the root of living faith which produces works is being distinguished from a dead and sterile conceptual orthodoxy: "So faith by itself, if it has no works, is dead. . . . For as the body apart from the spirit is dead, so faith apart from works is dead" (James 2:17, 26 [RSV]).

An unrepentant faith is a theoretical belief which originates outside the sphere of the Spirit's illumination in a heart which is still in darkness concerning its own need and the grace and grandeur of God. Paul points to incomplete realization of truth as the cause of the abuse of grace:

> Are we to continue in sin that grace may abound? By no means! How can we who died to sin still live in it? Do you not know that all of us who have been baptized into Christ Jesus were baptized into his death? . . . We know that our old self was crucified with him so that the sinful body might be destroyed, and we might no longer be enslaved to sin. For he who has died is freed from sin. (Romans 6:1–3, 6–7 [RSV]).

It is true that justification can only be appropriated on the ground of our union with Christ. But we cannot be in the light about our union with the perfect righteousness which covers our sin without simultaneously being in the light about the power available to transform our lives and displace our sin. We cannot be in union with half a Christ, as the Puritans would say. We must appropriate a whole Christ if we are to remain in light and thus in spiritual life.

There is a deep and indissoluble connection between our appropriation of justification and our experience of sanctification. On the one hand, the conscience cannot accept justification without sanctification. Assurance of justification which penetrates and cleanses our consciousness of guilt is impossible to obtain without an awareness that we are in some measure committed to progress in spiritual growth. This assurance increases as we move forward in sanctification and weakens or vanishes as we move away from the light of holiness (2 Peter 1:2–11). Though the attempt to claim justification without a clear commitment to sanctification outrages our conscience, we usually repress this from conscious awareness, and the resulting anxiety and insecurity create compulsive egocentric drives which aggravate the flesh instead of mortifying it. Thus the Protestant disease of cheap grace can produce some of the most selfish and contentious leaders and laypeople on earth, more difficult to bear in a state of grace than they would be in a state of nature.

On the other hand, the conscience cannot accept sanctification unless it is based on a foundation in justification. When this is attempted the resulting insecurity creates a luxuriant overgrowth of religious flesh as believers seek to build a holiness formidable enough to pacify their consciences and quiet their sense of alienation from God. Theoretically this should be a disorder limited to Catholics—medieval asceticism is the largest monument in history to the uneasy conscience which results when justification is misconstrued—but the large number of serious Protestants who are essentially insecure about their own justification makes it common in the rest of the church also.

As Romans 6 makes clear, the ground of sanctification is our union with Christ in his death and resurrection, in which the old nature was destroyed and a new nature created with the power to grow in newness of life. The Holy Spirit begins to apply this completed work in the believer's life at regeneration and continues it in a progressively enlarging sphere of renewal in the personality. This renewal will be complete only in the final resurrection.

Check off the assignments you've completed:

☐ Listened to Message 9

☐ Memorized Galatians 3:3–5

☐ Completed the exercises

☐ Read "Sanctification"

☐ Updated your prayer partner

Session

10
LIVING IN LIGHT OF THE CROSS

A disciple is not someone who's been perfected, but one who's learning that he's not perfect. Disciples are open to correction from others, even from people who aren't Christians. Because they are safe in the love of Jesus and his righteousness, they can bear the truth. The cross is large in their lives; they can take the honesty. The Holy Spirit can show them more of God's holiness and more of their own need without crushing them—because they have a Savior.

GOALS:

- To know that our calling as believers is to bring the gospel to others in love
- To understand what Christian growth ought to look like
- To recognize how Christian growth can often go wrong

>>> LISTEN TO MESSAGE 10

MESSAGE OUTLINE

1. "Going into foreign missions is like pouring Miracle-Gro on all your sins."

2. Odd pictures of discipleship

    a. Problem #1: An inadequate view of the flesh (sinful nature)

    b. Problem #2: An inadequate view of God's work in salvation (not my own efforts)

3. The primary ability of the new man is radical dependence

4. The Cross Chart: What Christian growth ought to look like
   (Note: See the end of this lesson for the Cross Chart.)

5. "If there was something you could change about me, what would it be?"

6. Trying to manage the pain of revealed sin—reveals pride and unbelief

7. A biblical view of discipleship: times of slow small steps and great leaps forward

8. Continuous renewal is a lifelong process

HOMEWORK

Name: Due:

Memorize:

> For the sinful nature desires what is contrary to the Spirit,
> and the Spirit what is contrary to the sinful nature. They are
> in conflict with each other, so that you do not do what you
> want.
>
> —*Galatians 5:17*

Go over the following section carefully before moving on to the exercises.

The power to transform us

Have you ever planted flowers or tomatoes in your yard? If you plant
a seed in the ground, what will transform it into a plant? What does it
take to change the seed into a beautiful flower? The answer is an outside power source: the sun. Of course, if you just threw your seed into
the backyard, you might get something, but probably only a scrawny
plant at best. So although the sun is the source of energy, you still have
to do your part. You till the ground, and fertilize it with Miracle-Gro;
you water your plants, perhaps even cover them, and generally keep a
close eye on them.

Now the question arises: did you cause the growth of the tomato plants?
No. You were not the outside source of power. You created a good envi-
ronment for that growth. But without the sun, even the water you give
to your plants will only cause them to rot. So if you want lots of fruit,
there is plenty for you to do. You have to participate in the process that
will eventually produce quality fruit, but you are not the power source
of that growth and transformation.

Relating this to sanctification, our power source is the Holy Spirit. He
is the one who transforms our hearts. However, we still participate in
that process. There are plenty of things for us to do: Bible study, prayer,
the Lord's Supper, fellowship, etc. But what we do does not produce

holiness in us. Only the Spirit produces holiness; hence "love," "joy," "peace," etc., are called the fruit of the Spirit (Galatians 5:22–23).

Furthermore, suppose that you plant your tomatoes in the shade, or perhaps a big weed grows up and blocks the sun. There may be some growth, but not much. So you need to make sure that nothing blocks the sun from your plants. In sanctification, that is called "repentance." The weeds and clouds are our sin, which block out the sun. Some sunlight will get through (on an ultraviolet level!) but not with full power. So one of the attractive aspects of repentance is that it leads to a greater infusion of the Holy Spirit's power. This being the case, why would we not want to repent? For many of us, it is because of our deep suspicion that God's love and ability to cleanse us do not run as deep as our sin. However, this is not the case, and God's love and his ability are always infinitely greater than our sin.

Complete the following questions and exercises:

1. Reflect on your teaching assignment (page 134), about the practical implications of sanctification by faith. Describe the personal illustration you used.

2. When you asked that person afterward to explain one practical application of sanctification by faith, what was the response? Write it below.

3. If you had the chance to do this exercise again, what would you do differently and why?

4. Overall, what impact do you think your discussion had? How much do you think the other person actually understood?

The Cross Chart, found at the end of this session (page 153), illustrates the fact that when we become Christians, we experience an unveiling of our sinfulness and the holiness of God (section 2 on the diagram). At the same time, we see that Jesus' blood covers our sin. Since the cross covers our sin, we can look at our sinful nature honestly. The more we grow, the more we see of our sins—and the more we see of Jesus.

As we continue to grow as Christians, we learn more about God's holiness—and thus, see more of our sin in the light of his holiness. On the chart, the gap between the wavy diagonal lines grows wider and wider. A significant problem arises, however, if our view of the cross remains the same as it was at conversion. A gap begins to appear between our view of the cross and our new awareness of sin. As the gap grows wider because of our growing awareness of our sin and of God's holiness, we're now faced with two options:

> A. We can see the cross as growing bigger and bigger, large enough to bridge the gap. We can cling to Jesus' righteousness and perfection. We can own up to our sin, repent, and refocus on our true identity in Christ (section 4).
> B. We can invent "another gospel" to protect ourselves and relieve our guilt.

As we forget about Jesus' righteousness, we devise strategies like blame-shifting, boasting, excuse-making, thinking of ourselves as a "special case," rationalizing, and lying to justify ourselves before God and other people (section 3). When we do this, we're adding to the cross, and Christ has become of no value to us (Galatians 5:2).

So are we going to defend ourselves and accuse others, or are we going to believe what the gospel says about us? In the pain of exposure, will we let the cross grow bigger (by clinging to Jesus' righteousness alone) and cover the gap that has come about because of the new awareness of our sin? Will we believe that the death of Christ is sufficient to cover all our sin? Or will our view of the sinful nature shrink, as we either falsify the record or defend ourselves? Will we invent "other gospels" to fill the gap in order to relieve our consciences?

5. Think about how you add to the cross (section 3). What's one way you try to do this through performance?

6. How do you add to the cross through dishonesty, or by defending yourself?

7. The Cross Chart teaches that as we mature we see more of our sin. Why is this necessary for genuine growth to take place?

8. However, knowledge of our sin alone does not transform us. What has to happen for growth to occur?

9. As we see more of our sin, what keeps us from despair and self-condemnation?

The Cross Chart also shows that we have a tendency to cover over things as we see more of our sin. We usually think that if a Christian is more aware of the love of Christ, more aware of her sins, and more loving toward others, she needs to be repenting less! As we grow, however, we actually face more opportunities to become self-righteous. If we become more self-righteous as we grow, we undermine the growth God has brought about.

As I grow, there are more opportunities for sin:

- My capacity for self-righteousness grows. I learn more, so I make fewer mistakes. I feel I have less to learn from other Christians, so I become unteachable, unreachable, and untouchable.
- My capacity for judging others grows because I see the faults of others more quickly. While I may see my own sins sooner, I also see the sins of others sooner. I become harsher and harder.
- I have a greater ability to cover over my sins. As I grow, I learn more about the extensiveness, characteristics, and manifestations of sin. I am in a better position to hide my sins. I learn to cover things up much better.
- My resistance to repentance may grow. I have more to lose in appearance and control. The more I grow, the more I have to lose.
- I have more success, so I begin believing that perhaps I've had something to do with it after all! I have more of Christ, so I'm more of a blessing to others. Deep down I start to think that something intrinsic to me produced my success.
- I have more opportunities to live out of the sinful nature. I'm wiser, so it becomes easier to do things on my own—without faith, prayer, or the Spirit.
- I grow in biblical knowledge. I've become more "right" in my knowledge. It's become easier to be self-righteous. I'm less likely to listen.
- I grow in experience. I've learned about many of the bad consequences of sin. As with example 7, I've developed an inability to listen—and a complete ignorance of that inability.
- Even as I grow, my life is always tending toward decay! But Jesus came for decaying sinners just like me!

10. In this lecture, the speaker says he was frail, blind, and unaware of his problem with anger. How did the Lord reveal his deep sin to him?

11. Ask your spouse or a close friend the question the speaker asked his spouse: "If there were one thing you could change about me, what would it be?" Write down all his or her comments here. (Note: Don't consider this a one-time-only assignment; look at it as a way of relating, of inviting insight from other people to deepen your repentance.)

12. How did you respond to your spouse or close friend after you received his or her answer? What did your response reveal about the sin still present in your life—and your awareness of it?

READ
The Rabbi's Heartbeat
— Brennan Manning, *Abba's Child*, pages 158–60, 169, 171

The evil operative within us resides in relentless self-absorption, in what Moore calls "our inescapable narcissism of consciousness." Therein lies the source of our cruelty, possessiveness, jealousy, and every species of malice. If we gloss over our selfishness and rationalize the evil within us, we can only pretend we are sinners and therefore only pretend we have been forgiven. A sham spirituality of pseudo-repentance and pseudo-bliss eventually fashions what modern psychiatry calls a borderline personality, in which appearances make up for reality.

Those who stop short of evil in themselves will never know what love is about. Unless and until we face our sanctimonious viciousness, we cannot grasp the meaning of the reconciliation Christ affected on Calvary's hill.

Humility, recovering alcoholics like to say, is stark raving honesty. Recovery from the disease cannot be initiated until the deadly denial dwelling in the subterranean personality of the drunk is exposed and acknowledged. He or she must hit bottom, arrive at the moment of truth when the pain it takes to hang on to the bottle becomes much greater than the pain it takes to let go. Similarly, we cannot receive what the crucified Rabbi has to give unless we admit our plight and stretch out our hands until our arms ache. . . .

Through His passion and death Jesus carried away the essential sickness of the human heart and broke forever the deadly grip of hypocrisy on our souls. He has robbed our loneliness of its fatal power by traveling Himself to the far reaches of loneliness ("My God, my God, why have You deserted Me?"). He has understood our ignorance, weakness, and foolishness and granted pardon to us all ("Forgive them, Father, they do not know what they are doing"). He has made His pierced heart a safe place for every defeated cynic, hopeless sinner, and self-loathing derelict across the bands of time. God reconciled all things, everything in heaven and everything on earth, when He made peace by His death on the cross (Colossians 1:20).

The Cross reveals that Jesus has conquered sin and death and that nothing, absolutely nothing, can separate us from the love of Christ. Neither the imposter nor the pharisee, neither the lack of awareness nor the lack of passion, neither the negative judgments of others nor the debased perception of ourselves, neither our scandalous past nor our uncertain future, neither the power struggles in the church nor the tensions in our marriage, nor fear, guilt, shame, self-hatred, nor even death can tear us away from the love of God, made visible in Jesus the Lord.

Listening to the faint heartbeat of the dying Rabbi is a powerful stimulus to the recovery of passion. It is a sound like no other.

The Crucified says, "Confess your sin so that I may reveal Myself to you as lover, teacher, and friend, that fear may depart and your heart can stir once again with passion." His word is addressed both to those filled with a sense of self-importance and to those crushed with a sense of self-worthlessness. Both are preoccupied with themselves. Both claim a godlike status, because their full attention is riveted either on their prominence or their insignificance. They are isolated and alienated in their self-absorption.

The release from chronic egocentricity starts with letting Christ love them where they are. . . .

Heart to heart. The Rabbi implores, "Don't you understand that discipleship is not about being right or being perfect or being efficient? It's all about the way you live with each other." In every encounter we either give life or we drain it. There is no neutral exchange. We enhance human dignity, or we diminish it. The success or failure of a given day is measured by the quality of our interest and compassion toward those around us. . . .

Wise men and women have long held that happiness lies in being yourself without inhibitions. Let the Great Rabbi hold you silently against His heart. In learning who He is, you will find out who you are: Abba's child in Christ our Lord.

DIAGRAM: THE CROSS CHART

©2012 World Harvest Mission

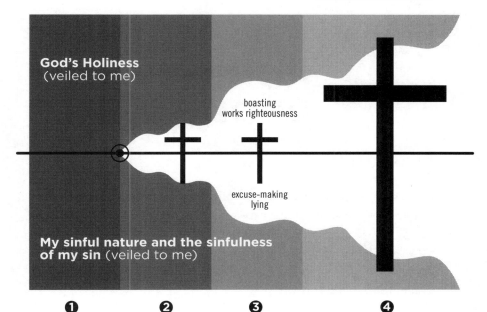

❶	**❷**	**❸**	**❹**
Before Conversion	**After Conversion**	**Adjusting the Record**	**Boasting in the Cross!**
The holiness of God, my sinful nature, and the sinfulness of my sin are veiled to me.	I have a limited, fluctuating, but growing awareness of both God's holiness and my sinfulness.	I resort to dishonesty and performance to bridge the gap when my belief in the gospel does not keep pace with what I know of God's holiness and my sin.	As I daily believe the gospel, the cross bridges the gap; I rest in my identity in Christ and his righteousness, which enables me to own up to God's holiness and my sinfulness without trying to adjust the record. Now, by faith, I am empowered and freed up to love God and my neighbor.

Check off the assignments you've completed:

- ☐ Listened to Message 10
- ☐ Memorized Galatians 5:17
- ☐ Completed the exercises
- ☐ Read "The Rabbi's Heartbeat"
- ☐ Updated your prayer partner

Session

11 HUMILITY AND BROKENNESS

This lesson is about practicing humility, not learning about humility. Perhaps you feel as if you have more than enough humility; if so, consider this session an opportunity to get more material to teach to others. However, there may be a few of us who have a habitual problem with lack of humility—or at least friends and family who have a problem with our lack of humility.

GOALS:

- To recognize and personally apply the truth that God resists our pride and gives grace as we are humbled
- To understand that this grace is especially evident in how we use our tongues

>>> LISTEN TO MESSAGE 11

MESSAGE OUTLINE

1. Luther on the Bible (James 3–4)

2. Grace is for the humble

    a. The work of God's Spirit

    b. Grace is for sinners

    c. "How is it with your soul?"

3. Grace shows in the way you use your tongue

4. Learn to love the weak and needy

5. The threefold solution

HOMEWORK

Name: Due:

Memorize:

> But he gives us more grace. That is why Scripture says:
> "God opposes the proud but gives grace to the humble."
> —*James 4:6*

Complete the following questions and exercises:

1. Write down a habitual surface sin in your life, perhaps an area of your life to which you have not addressed and applied the gospel. A surface sin is a sin that can be seen by others, not a hidden, heart sin. For some examples, consider the following list:

- I'm usually demanding or intense with my spouse, kids, or close friends.
- I worry a lot; anxiety clouds my conversations.
- I'm very ambitious and tend to run over people.
- I overeat.
- I lust over magazines at the supermarket (I want the women portrayed there/I want to look like the women portrayed there).
- I withdraw from people I don't like; I attack people I don't like.
- I am Ms. Scrooge or Mr. Shop-till-I-drop when it comes to money and possessions.
- I'm an angry person (those closest to me know this).
- I'm disrespectful to those in authority over me.
- I have a hard time completing projects; I tend to be lazy.
- I'm bitter over past relationships and events in my life (ask me about them if you don't believe me).
- I don't forgive others easily; I complain and gossip about others.
- I overwork; I'm generally impatient and irritable.
- I am often harsh, and do not really listen to people.
- I often "correct" people, and give them "suggestions" for improvement.
- I often defend myself.

2. Write down two recent instances of this surface sin. Include where these incidents occurred, the various circumstances, and who was involved.

It's important, to identify the heart sins behind our surface sins. We need to identify what's driving our hearts, so that we can apply the gospel more profoundly, and deepen our repentance in the process. Essentially, what drives our hearts is unbelief. However, unbelief is a broad category. Therefore, we need to understand the specific content of our unbelief. The following are just two examples of heart sins that lie behind certain surface sins.

- Perhaps you chose the example "I am often harsh, and do not really listen to people."

Behind harshness is a deep-seated arrogance—an awareness of, and confidence in, my so-called great abilities and successes. "People don't understand as quickly as I do. People ought to know better. So many people have really big problems." I am self-righteous and have very little sense that I am a sinner. My belief is, "I am not a big sinner. I am right." I am self-centered and unconcerned with others. These are heart sins, idols, forms of unbelief. I've turned away from Christ's righteousness as my only righteousness. I've forsaken God in favor of my own idols and strategies. Because I'm right, I have little ability to listen. Why listen when I know the right answer? Because of my confidence in my abilities, I think that others are slow talkers and slow thinkers. Why not just cut them short? I condemn others because I have lost touch with the gospel.

- Or, you may have chosen "I lust over magazines at the supermarket (I want the women portrayed there/I want to look like the women portrayed there)."

Behind this surface sin is a lustful and prideful heart. This lust is sexual desire out of control and out of bounds. Here the passion driving my heart is a passion in the wrong direction. When my desires and passions are going out of bounds, it's clear that my passion isn't for God. The sin isn't sexual desire itself, but rather that desire going out of bounds. When I lust, I believe that this will bring me relief (however temporary) from pain, frustration, meaninglessness, and boredom. I trust it to bring blessing, pleasure, and intimacy that only Jesus can give. There's also a deep-rooted pride and arrogance behind sexual lust. For men, this pride says, "I'm so great that these women would want me." For women, this pride says, "Look how many people would admire me if only I looked like this."

3. As you consider your surface sin, what root or heart sins lie beneath that sin? Here are some further questions to help you identify heart sins: Do you desire control, peace, respect, or love? Do you trust your own righteousness or capabilities? Do you fear failure, exposure, or rejection?

Session 11 159

4. How do these heart sins masquerade as "good news"? In other
   words, what do they give you or promise you?

Once we've identified the specific areas of unbelief driving our surface
sins, it's easier to see how the gospel can apply. In contrast to idols, the
gospel really does give us what it promises—intimacy, pleasure, joy,
reputation, love, peace. So, for example, when I am harsh and have
little sense that I'm a sinner, the gospel tells me that I am the chief of
sinners; I don't have it all together; I have a log (and not a speck) in my
eye. Essentially, *I am not right*. I need to make Christ's righteousness
my rest and delight. When I receive these truths, I recognize that I'm
often wrong, blind, and deceived—hence my inability to hear what
others have to say. I no longer have to be intent on proving my own
righteousness. From this position of repentance and faith, I can move
toward people with greater humility, compassion, and understanding.
I will become more tender, now that I am at the foot of the cross.

Similarly, the gospel speaks powerfully to my lustful heart. Jesus can
give me all the intimacy I need. Jesus' power enables me to delay gratifi-
cation, and even to suffer. The gospel can relieve my frustration, meaninglessness, and boredom. It also speaks to the entrenched pride and
arrogance that lie behind sexual lust. My desire for adoration, or my
belief that others will adore me, is in direct conflict with the gospel,
since worship is directed toward myself and not Christ. I can repent of
my lack of worship and passion for God. Out of this repentance and

faith comes the ability to love people, instead of using them for my own pleasure.

5.   In contrast to the heart sins you described in your answers to questions 3 and 4, what can the gospel give you that is real, beautiful, lovely, wonderful, powerful, and lasting? How does the gospel speak to those sins you described?

6.   As you begin to experience the outworking of repentance and faith in the gospel, in what ways do you think your outward behavior should begin to change?

7. Give your answers to questions 1–6 to your prayer partner, so that he or she can pray about these areas. Check the following box when you have notified your prayer partner. □

8. One great hindrance to humility is self-pity. Often, instead of grieving and repenting for our sins, we lapse into self-pity. Read James 4:9–10, and describe what you think is the difference between the grieving James talks about and self-pity.

Self-pity is a serious concern. Many of us indulge in it far more than we realize. There's a subtle pleasure in it, but we need to recognize that it's a major struggle. There's something very seductive about self-pity, since we often prefer it to the gospel. At the core of self-pity are pride and self-justification. There's a profound self-righteousness and sense of entitlement behind self-pity. Perhaps even unconsciously, we enjoy a victim-martyr status based on the lie that God has not been good to us: "Life is so unfair!" The self-pitying victim believes he hasn't gotten something he's entitled to. However, we cannot mix self-pity with the gospel. They are like oil and water—they don't mix. We can have one or the other, but not both.

9. What are two areas of disappointment in your life where you tend to fall into self-pity? What do you think is behind your self-pity?

10. How is the gospel "good news" for you in such a struggle? Be specific.

11. Describe three truths about the gospel that have become more precious to you, making you less afraid to ask God to humble you and give you a spirit of brokenness.

READ

The Great Sin

— C. S. Lewis, *Mere Christianity*, pages 108–12, 114

Today I come to that part of Christian morals where they differ most sharply from all other morals. There is one vice of which no man in the world is free; which every one in the world loathes when he sees it in someone else; and of which hardly any people, except Christians, ever imagine that they are guilty themselves. I have heard people admit that they are bad-tempered, or that they cannot keep their heads about girls or drink, or even that they are cowards. I do not think I have ever heard anyone who was not a Christian accuse himself of this vice. And at the same time I have very seldom met anyone, who was not a Christian, who showed the slightest mercy to it in others. There is no fault which makes a man more unpopular, and no fault which we are more unconscious of in ourselves. And the more we have it ourselves, the more we dislike it in others.

The vice I am talking of is Pride or Self-Conceit: and the virtue opposite to it, in Christian morals, is called Humility. You may remember, when I was talking about sexual morality, I warned you that the centre of Christian morals did not lie there. Well, now, we have come to the centre. According to Christian teachers, the essential vice, the utmost evil, is Pride. Unchastity, anger, greed, drunkenness, and all that, are mere fleabites in comparison: it was through Pride that the devil became the devil: Pride leads to every other vice: it is the complete anti-God state of mind.

Does this seem to you exaggerated? If so, think it over. I pointed out a moment ago that the more pride one had, the more one disliked pride in others. In fact, if you want to find out how proud you are the easiest way is to ask yourself, "How much do I dislike it when other people snub me, or refuse to take any notice of me, or shove their oar in, or patronise me, or show off?" The point is that each person's pride is in competition with every one else's pride. It is because I wanted to be the big noise at the party that I am so annoyed at someone else being the big noise. Two of a trade never agree. Now what you want to get clear is that Pride is essentially competitive—is competitive by its very nature—while the other vices are competitive only, so to speak, by accident. Pride gets no pleasure out of having something, only out of having more of it than the next man. We say that people are proud of being rich, or clever, or good-looking, but they are not. They are proud of being richer, or cleverer, or better-looking than others. If every one else became equally rich, or clever, or good-looking there would be nothing to be proud about.

It is the comparison that makes you proud: the pleasure of being above the rest. Once the element of competition has gone, pride has gone. That is why I say that Pride is essentially competitive in a way the other vices are not....

The Christians are right: it is Pride which has been the chief cause of misery in every nation and every family since the world began. Other vices may sometimes bring people together: you may find good fellowship and jokes and friendliness among drunken people or unchaste people. But Pride always means enmity—it *is* enmity. And not only enmity between man and man, but enmity to God.

In God you come up against something which is in every respect immeasurably superior to yourself. Unless you know God as that—and, therefore, know yourself as nothing in comparison—you do not know God at all. As long as you are proud you cannot know God. A proud man is always looking down on things and people: and, of course, as long as you are looking down, you cannot see some thing that is above you.

That raises a terrible question. How is it that people who are quite obviously eaten up with Pride can say they believe in God and appear to themselves very religious? I am afraid it means they are worshipping an imaginary God. They theoretically admit themselves to be nothing in the presence of this phantom God, but are really all the time imagining how He approves of them and thinks them far better than ordinary people: that is, they pay a pennyworth of imaginary humility to Him and get out of it a pound's worth of Pride towards their fellow-men. I suppose it was of those people Christ was thinking when He said that some would preach about Him and cast out devils in His name, only to be told at the end of the world that He had never known them. And any of us may at any moment be in this death-trap. Luckily, we have a test. Whenever we find that our religious life is making us feel that we are good—above all, that we are better than someone else—I think we may be sure that we are being acted on, not by God, but by the devil. The real test of being in the presence of God is that you either forget about yourself altogether or see yourself as a small, dirty object. It is better to forget about yourself altogether.

It is a terrible thing that the worst of all the vices can smuggle itself into the very centre of our religious life. . . . The devil laughs. He is perfectly content to see you becoming chaste and brave and self-controlled pro-vided, all the time, he is setting up in you the Dictatorship of Pride—just as he would be quite content to see your chilblains cured if he was allowed, in return, to give you cancer. For Pride is spiritual cancer: it eats up the very possibility of love, or contentment, or even common sense. . . .

Do not imagine that if you meet a really humble man he will be what most people call "humble" nowadays: he will not be a sort of greasy, smarmy person, who is always telling you that, of course, he is nobody. Probably all you will think about him is that he seemed a cheerful, intelligent chap who took a real interest in what you said to him. If you do dislike him it will be because you feel a little envious of anyone who seems to enjoy life so easily. He will not be thinking about humility: he will not be thinking about himself at all.

If anyone would like to acquire humility, I can, I think, tell him the first step. The first step is to realise that one is proud. And a biggish step, too. At least, nothing whatever can be done before it. If you think you are not conceited, it means you are very conceited indeed.

Check off the assignments you've completed:

☐ Listened to Message 11

☐ Memorized James 4:6

☐ Completed the exercises

☐ Read "The Great Sin"

☐ Updated your prayer partner

12

THE PROPULSION OF GRACE

The renewal that God is bringing into your life leads somewhere. There's a push behind it. There's propulsion in it. For some of you, that may mean missions. For others of you, it may mean a new ministry right where you are. For yet others it may mean not an official ministry but picking up a family responsibility you've struggled with, or accepting opportunities to love difficult people around you. There is a kingdom, and God has a call upon your life.

GOALS:

- To see that the gospel is not just for ourselves, but is also meant to be given away to others
- To grab hold of God's plan for his kingdom
- To realize that the Holy Spirit equips us to be used in many wonderful ways

>>>LISTEN TO MESSAGE 12

MESSAGE OUTLINE

1. A difficult time of ministry: "What am I doing here?"

2. Heart renewal and kingdom work

3. The Spirit moves you out

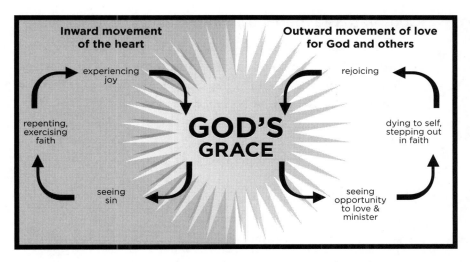

4. Where does your competence for ministry come from (2 Corinthians 2)?

HOMEWORK

Name: Due:

Memorize:

"But you will receive power when the Holy Spirit comes on you; and you will be my witnesses in Jerusalem, and in all Judea and Samaria, and to the ends of the earth."

—*Acts 1:8*

Complete the following questions and exercises:

1. The speaker describes his battle of faith in Russia, and his struggle to believe that God could and would use him in those circumstances. Using this as an example, describe one area where the "battle of faith" lies for you in your present circumstances.

2. Read 2 Corinthians 5:14. What is it that drives Paul? Explain your answer.

3. Where would you like to see the love of Christ work itself out in your life? Give two examples.

4. When the speaker took his son to Siberia, he messed up; his son saw his worry and failure. How do you respond when you fail in front of someone? What does it feel like? What does it look like to others in your thoughts and speech?

5. Describe two areas of your life where you're playing it safe or deliberately avoiding God's call because of worries, concern that your failures will be exposed, laziness, fear of weakness, sense of incompetence, etc.

As the gospel changes us, it begins to work itself out in every part of our lives. We're no longer ruled by fear of others but by the love of Christ. It changes how we respond to people—especially people who aren't like us, or who don't yet know Jesus.

6. Name two people who upset you because of their lifestyles, behavior, speech, or values. (Use initials, not real or full names.)

   Person 1:   Person 2:

7. What bothers or offends you about them, and why?

8. How are you nonetheless like them?

9. How can the gospel change your heart, and your actions, toward these people?

The gospel that changes and renews us, always pushes us out into the world in loving service and sacrifice. We're to remember that the Father's heart is not just turned toward us, but also toward those who are lost. The Son, the great missionary, did not send messages, training, resources, or messengers from his home. Rather, he became one of us in the incarnation. Now he calls us to join him in his heart for the world.

There are at least five things we can do to be a part of reaching the world for Christ. We are to:

- Pray (Romans 15:30)
- Give (Philippians 4:14–19)
- See (John 4:35–38)
- Send (John 17:18)
- Go (Matthew 28:18–20)

10. *Pray.* For what missionaries, people, or works are you praying in a committed and ongoing way? What is God calling you to do in prayer?

11. *Give.* How are you committed to using your resources and money to help reach the world for Jesus? How is God calling you to give further?

12. *See.* How are you learning to "see" the needs of the world outside your own country—people, books, conferences, perhaps short-term missions work? What opportunities should you pursue?

13. *Send.* Releasing is part of sending. The Father sent the Son; the Son sent his disciples. Likewise, we are to be a part of his sending by encouraging, releasing, and supporting others who go—friends, church members, leaders, and family. Who do you need to release, send, or encourage going—and in what ways?

14. *Go.* We all benefit from asking ourselves the question "Should I go?" Even if God's answer is a confirmation of your present calling, asking the question in faith can't hurt. So ask yourself, "Where would you have me to go, Lord? Where should I serve? Are you preparing and calling me to service abroad?" Write below what you sense God is saying to you.

15. Is there someone who doesn't know Jesus whom you sense the Lord is leading you to befriend? What are some practical steps you can take to move toward him or her?

READ

The Love of Christ Compels Us

—Jack Miller, *The Heart of a Servant Leader,* pages 70–76

Perhaps you don't drift the way I do, but I constantly forget the deep hole of depravity from which the Lord's mighty love rescued me. Drifting does not take any effort at all—just stop cultivating the knowledge of Christ, and the evil current of secularism does the rest. All passion for the lost seems increasingly a fading memory: Jesus weeping over Jerusalem or Paul willing to be cursed for the sake of his countrymen, become very remote to the point of being unreal. I entreat you to pray for me that my memory of my former lost condition will be fresh and green and that I will have the Spirit teach me a second lesson. This one follows from the former lesson. It is a right sense of obligation based upon a clear understanding of the purpose for which we are saved.

We have had an incredible rescue from lostness. What a debt we owe for this rescue and its great cost to our Lord! But how much our obligation is increased by our privileged destiny. Our pilgrimage will climax with our coming to resemble Christ exactly—the flawless image of the Lord. Now I'm sure every true Christian agrees that the ultimate goal of our lives is to become Christlike. But is the glory of it understood; the privilege, the honor, and the compelling obligation? Well, we are stirred to think about it now and then. Sometimes we hunger for the hour of our glorification in the image of the Son of God. But it's a longing that fades. Our minds are lazy; busy lifestyles have little place for deep thinking about the very reason for our existence.

Too, we assume that we are more in touch with our destiny than we are. We know that we have some love for God and for people. And to love God and our neighbor as ourselves is the essence of being Christlike. Are we not already, then, reasonably far down the road toward Christlikeness? It is easily said by us. We have taught it to others and been praised for our teaching of the centrality of Christlike love. Why then study, pursue, and long for that which we seem to have substantially attained already?

Nevertheless, the Spirit of grace woos us from self-congratulation. We go to the work and find we have little power to do it God's way and see God's results. We sense our lack of grace and the weakening of fellowship with the Father. We face a temptation. We feel the power of jealousy, lust, hatred, or despair and realize unexpectedly how unlike Christ we really are. He lived in perfect submission to the missionary will of the Father. He did not choose to be in control of his own life. In the hour of fiery trial he cried, "Not my will, but your will be done!"

But in my inner heart I find that my ego constantly wants to take control away from the Father. One of the deepest compulsions of my flesh is to say to my Father, "Let me be in control. Let my will be done now. I'll do your will later." Two nights ago I had to confess to Rose Marie at midnight that my soul was carrying all kinds of burdens, that I was inwardly trying to be in control of many things by worrying about them. Led by the Spirit, I said, "Please pray for me! I'm carrying all kinds of weight and anxieties tonight. I did not know it, but I've been trying to be in control of my life, work, and future. But I'm repenting of wanting to be the Holy Spirit. Ask the Lord to cleanse me!" Her effective praying led to a cleansing and release for my needy soul. It was not that all my cares immediately fell away. But the good beginning was granted by the Father. I rested in the promise of the Spirit's presence and not in my own performance—or in the redemptive power of my anxieties. I also gained a clearer understanding of what it means to be like Jesus, my elder brother, and the joyous obligation my oneness with him imparts to me.

Christ's missionary passion

The Lord in his life on earth had a single-minded passion for doing the saving will of God. In his incarnation and atonement he provided the "alien righteousness" that became the good news for sinners. He came without self-interest. His only purpose was "to seek and to save that which was lost" (Luke 19:10) because this was his Father's will. The house of salvation was opened to all nations through Jesus' one great work of atoning sacrifice (John 2:19; 4:34; 5:36; 14:31; 17:4, 18; 20:21).

Our minds may be like well-arranged file cabinets or overturned waste-baskets. But it's all small stuff, pitifully shriveled if it is disconnected from Jesus' one great master work. His joyous obligation concentrated all his powers. Note how his public ministry begins. He forgets himself. He cleanses the temple with holy indignation. He says, "How dare you turn my Father's house into a market!" (John 2:16). Why the wrath? It was neither polite nor politic. But Jesus knows only the Father's will. The Father has purposed that his house be a salvation house for the Gentile sinners, the unwashed, the "all nations" promised to Abraham and made the subjects of Jesus' Great Commission (Genesis 12:3; Matthew 28:19).

What was going on? What stirred the fierce anger of Jesus? Listen, dear brother. Here is the core issue. The church of God again and again gets in the way of "the nations" coming to salvation by its busyness and business—and it forgets this master purpose. We forget: I forget; you forget; the church forgets. The court filled with money changers and the market for the sale of animals was the welcome court of the nations. It had been built by the people of God anticipating the fulfillment of Isaiah 56:6–8. It was the welcome court for the lost, the missionary part of the temple complex, the setting for sinners to taste of his redeeming grace.

My own heart is stirred deeply by the Spirit of Jesus as I write these words. My mind's eye can see Jesus standing there. He sternly takes it all in, the haggling over money, the bleating of the sheep, and the confusion of the Gentile worshipers. No one welcomes these strangers; no one teaches them the promises of grace or calls them to brokenness over their sins. Jesus' great heart is deeply grieved. He moves through the tumultuous scene, making a whip of cords, and driving "all from the temple area." The sheer violence of the action astonishes me. No wonder the disciples for once remember a Scripture verse describing Jesus' act: "Zeal for your house has eaten me up" (John 2:16, 17). Jesus' soul is full of salvation fire, and he will not tolerate obstacles being put in the way of recovery of the lost.

Soren Kierkegaard once said that "purity of heart is to will one thing." His statement is not true at all if that one thing is to do our own will. Then we end up little Hitlers or Jeffrey Dahmers. But when by the

Spirit's aid we will God's saving purpose, when we reject our own will to do this, we grow in purity of heart. We may even burn with holy indignation.

Compassion and a heart for the lost

Rose Marie and I took a walk on the beautiful beach at Cabo Pino (Cape of Pines). It's about as lovely a beach as any in Europe, a favorite spot for walking breaks. While there we found ourselves in the presence of a number of nude men deliberately putting their bodies on display. We ignored them, just talking together as we walked near the sea's edge. We looked down or across the Med or toward the mountains of Africa. But one middle-aged man, completely naked, walked toward us as we tried to avoid him, and then he determinedly walked between us. It was a willful attempt to force his lifestyle on us, a crude attempt to cause offense, and something of a crusading attempt to force his evil exhibitionism on us. He was sold out to his own will and glorying in it. I was angry and upset. I stayed that way for a time, until I remembered my obligation to Jesus and his will. He had made me debt-free from sin and guilt. But as a debt-free child of the King I now had a new debt, to love others as Christ loved me. I owed this love debt to Jesus and to these men lost in their rebellion. I then prayed for them, forgiving them, blessing them, and asking Christ to save them. It also cleared the air of its poison.

Rose Marie said, "Probably we are the only ones ever to pray for these men." Poor lost souls, the Lord's missionary Spirit enabled us to see them with the Father's compassion, a true miracle of grace because my anger at the beginning was unholy. It came from a divided heart, a heart half-committed to Rose Marie's and my well-being and half-committed to the will of our missionary God. Think of it this way. The message of the cross takes away the burden of guilt and sin, removes forever the divine wrath from us; then it also takes away the heavy burden of our selfishness and self-preoccupation. I am offended because a beautiful beach has been taken over by homosexuals from Northern Europe. I think about what I have lost, about my feelings concerning their blatant self-assertion, etc. But the Holy Spirit rebukes me. He questions,

"Where will they spend eternity? You give up your daily walk on a lovely beach, but they will perish forever unless they repent." Then he leads me to repentance, to will one will, to taste the sweetness of his mighty love and to long for these men to experience the same self-forgetting peace.

Kingdom-oriented prayer

What is my method in praying? Am I a prayer warrior? Not at all. Rather, the older I get the more I know how hard it is to pray. Therefore, what I do is to try to maintain, as much as I can, regular prayer for all our missionaries, home staff, pastors in the churches, and especially for a core group of World Harvest Mission churches and pastors. But my praying is always drifting, marred by coldness, forgetting and apathy. Accordingly, I need to press forward or my prayer life will shrivel to nothing. One way the Lord helps me do my prayer work is by taking an individual missionary couple and praying for them intensively for two weeks or more, sometimes a month.

The effectiveness of this approach can be seen in several ways. Altogether apart from what it accomplishes in their lives, the practice of praying for them trains my mind to keep on praying for them after the concentrated period is completed. In fact, it may mean that the concentrated prayer will keep right on. That's my hope! This approach also clears my vision, especially my sensitivity to God's will for the ones being prayed for. For instance, I have prayed for you, and for myself that the truths of redemption would become deeply felt realities in our inmost being, that we would hate the sin of apathy in ourselves and others, and passionately love the lost with boldness, tenderness, and brokenness.

I want the Spirit to grace me with much patience, a willingness to take each small step necessary to make friends with the lost person, and then boldly stand before the heart's door and knock, there to stand with tears before the person's inner citadel and plead for the lost one to grab hold of the only salvation there is. The Father must give much new grace if this is to happen. I am often so far from this kind of total commitment to the Lord Jesus. Pray for me, my brother, pray for me.

Check off the assignments you've completed:

☐ Listened to Message 12

☐ Memorized Acts 1:8

☐ Completed the exercises

☐ Read "The Love of Christ Compels Us"

☐ Updated your prayer partner

13

THE LIBERATED CONSCIENCE

If we move the center of our life out from under the gospel—under its acceptance, under its forgiveness, under its power—we will have conscience problems. Very often, the first way we move away from the gospel is by living for other people's approval.

GOALS:

- To understand how a clear conscience leads to bold love
- To see how our relationships are hindered when our conscience is not clear
- To know that the Spirit desires to empower our love by freeing our conscience

>>> LISTEN TO MESSAGE 13

MESSAGE OUTLINE

1. How the gospel liberates the conscience

2. Why we often have a guilty conscience

    a. Moving from under the gospel to under human approval (Galatians 1:26)

b. Failing the law of love

c. Accusations by Satan

3. How to maintain a good conscience

 a. 1 John 3:16

 b. Abigail's example

HOMEWORK

Name: Due:

Memorize:

> How much more then will the blood of Christ, who through the eternal Spirit offered himself unblemished to God, cleanse our consciences from the acts that lead to death, so that we may serve the living God!
> —*Hebrews 9:14*

Go over the following section carefully before moving on to the exercises.

A clear conscience

The subject of the liberated conscience is closely related to what we've been studying in this course. Think of a clear conscience as one that does not live under condemnation and accusation. A clear conscience means we "draw near to God . . . in full assurance of faith" (Hebrews 10:22–24), deeply sensing his love and favor, and relying on his promises to be our strength and security. A clear conscience means that we're no longer under the burden of self-condemnation and sense of worthlessness that drives us to suck approval from others and demand their applause for our successes. Rather, we're assured of our identity as sons and daughters, our worth in Christ, and the security of a wonderful relationship we can never lose.

As we trust the blood of Christ to cover our sins, failures, weaknesses, and inadequacies, and as we trust his righteousness to clothe us in beauty, we're free to love people with daring selflessness. We no longer need allies in cleansing our conscience, because our conscience has already been so thoroughly cleansed by Christ. No longer must we manipulate, demand, or coax them to say or do things to assure us that we are good and worthy people. Nor do we need to defend ourselves, withdraw from them, or hurt them for attacking or undermining our goodness and worth. As Jesus increasingly becomes the only one who cleanses and measures our conscience, we're free to seek and to serve people—for what they need, not for what we think we need.

As we step out to love, we will be confident of our Father's partnership. We'll never love others well unless our conscience is good and clean— unless we're living under the gospel. A clear conscience enables us to be vulnerable and move toward people with bold love. Without this foundation, we'll be timid and unwilling to risk our safety and security to face possible rejection. As Paul notes, love comes from a pure heart, a good conscience, and a sincere faith (1 Timothy 1:5).

Complete the following questions and exercises:

1. In the message, the speaker talks about needing the bread of the Holy Spirit more than anything else. How are you growing in dependence on the Spirit? Are you having more desire for the Spirit to show you your sinful fears and offensive ways, and for him to cleanse you? Why or why not?

2. Do you have any negative or fearful attitudes about the Spirit, especially as you ask him to show you what you're like, to cleanse you, and to give you a spirit of brokenness?

3. The speaker frequently refers to her desire to control her life, and how instead she needs the Spirit to be in control and orchestrate her day. Where's your desire for control most evident on a daily basis? How does it inevitably frustrate and disappoint you?

4. As you think over the last few months, do you have any new insights into how you act, speak, and think (at home, at work, with your spouse, kids, friends, etc.)? How is it tied to your need for approval?

5. Choose two people you believe you need to love in a far greater or better way than you've done in the past. (Use initials, not real or full names.)

    Person 1:   Person 2:

6. What it would mean for you to let go of what's safe and secure in the above relationships? In what ways could you put their interests above your own (Philippians 2:4), and lay down your life for your brother or sister (1 John 3:16)?

    In the spaces below, describe what it might look like, to love these two people vulnerably, selflessly, and boldly, in tangible and practical ways. Don't merely write what you could do or want to do, but rather, what it would take great faith for you to do. Envision what God could do through you in these relationships.
    Person 1:

Person 2:

7. Write down the real purpose of loving these people in the manner you described in your answer to question 6.

8. In what ways might you be timid, unmotivated, fearful, or even angry about loving these people in the ways you've described? Why?

9. Apply the gospel to these two relationships. What truths and promises do you need to remind yourself of, as you move toward them? What lies do you need to stop believing? Describe how your heart needs to be repositioned toward these two people.

   Person 1:

   Person 2:

10. Keeping in mind the importance of a clear conscience, how you have depended in the past on what these two people have done or said? How has their good or bad opinion of you mattered? In what ways have you looked for their approval?

11. How does moving away from the need for approval allow you to love others more fully? Give an example.

12. In what ways do you despise or dismiss people who bother you? How have you distanced yourself or desired to punish them because of the way they've treated you?

Set your heart toward loving these two people in the ways you've described. Be willing to continue the journey and process of loving them. Pray that the Spirit would empower you, cleanse you, assure you of your adoption as God's child, and give you faith to step out in selfless love. Ask your prayer partner to join you.

READ

The Transforming Power of the Gospel

—Steven L. Childers, *Reformed Quarterly*, Fall 1995

I am a recovering Pharisee. I love the praise of man more than the praise of God. I naturally substitute a knowledge about God and godliness for truly knowing God. I can defend the truths of the Gospel, but I often fail to experience its transforming power in my life.

The depth of my Pharisaism was exposed several years ago when I co-taught a Doctor of Ministry class. During one session, my colleague realized how many of the pastors and Christian leaders in our class seemed discouraged and spiritually defeated. I, too, was struggling—just doing a great job of disguising it in front of the class.

Observing the pain all around him, he took me aside and suggested I divide the class into groups of three and lead them in sharing the Gospel with each other. I was stunned. "Why?" I wondered. Did he think some of these people weren't really Christians?

As he explained, however, I realized how faulty my reasoning had been. I had assumed that the Gospel was for non-Christians alone and had little or no relevance to the Christian life once someone was converted. I began learning that day that the Gospel is not just a gate I must pass through one time, but a path I should walk each day of my life.

It's a painfully common story. We begin the Christian life well, but gradually find ourselves increasingly experiencing little or no true spiritual transformation.

The good news for Christians is that a divine remedy for our cold and hardened hearts is available! And that remedy is found in the transforming power of the Gospel, the goal of which is not just our regeneration but also our transformation into the image of Christ. Its purpose is not merely forgiveness but change into true worshippers of God and authentic lovers of people.

However, we often reduce the Gospel to "God's plan of salvation" for lost people to be saved from sin's penalty, not realizing that it is also

"God's plan of salvation" for Christians to be saved from sin's power. The same Gospel message that saves sinners also sanctifies the saints.

In order to understand more fully how the Gospel saves us as believers and thereby changes our hearts, we must first learn to reject the counterfeit spiritual remedies being freely dispensed today.

The Nominalist response to a lack of spiritual transformation in the heart of a Christian is to say, "Don't worry about it. That's just part of being human. Don't you know we're under grace and not law?" But the Bible teaches that any long-term friendship with sin should alert us to the deadness of our hearts and, perhaps, to our unsaved state.

The second prescription we must reject is that of the Passivist, who believes that, as Christians, we make no real contribution to our spiritual transformation except to relinquish control of our lives to God. To solve our spiritual battles we just need to "let go and let God." This view can easily lead us to spend our entire lives chasing one false hope or experience after another in search of "something more" to make our faith more fulfilling. Instead of seeking "something more," we must learn to understand and draw upon all that we already have "in Christ" (Colossians 2:9, 10).

A final false solution is that of the Moralist, whose motto is, "Just try harder!" The view is packaged to look a lot more sophisticated and spiritual than that, but if you listen closely you still hear one core message: try harder to spend more time in the Word and prayer—try harder to be a better witness—try harder not to be angry or worried—try harder to be a more loving spouse or parent. We can hear only so many motivating pep talks before we find ourselves lapsing into either a lifestyle of spiritual denial or despair over the glaring lack of inward reality in our lives. The Apostle Paul wrote, "Are you so foolish? After beginning with the Spirit, are you now trying to attain your goal by human effort?" (Galatians 3:3).

The reason the above prescriptions inevitably leave people unchanged and in either denial or despair is because they all bypass the heart. Our root problem is not external or behavioral; it is a problem of the heart.

True spirituality is not only a matter of the mind and the will; it is also a matter of the heart. In his classic work *Religious Affections*, Jonathan Edwards writes, "A person who has a knowledge of doctrine and theology only—without religious affection—has never engaged in true religion."

One of the primary reasons my heart is not more transformed is because I have allowed what the Puritans called "the affections of my heart" to be captured by idols that grip me and steal my heart affection away from God.

The modern idols that capture our hearts' affections today are things like approval, reputation, possessions, power, pleasure, control, relationships, sex, or money. When we allow the affections of our hearts to be captured and corrupted by these idols, the outcome is always the same—a lack of God's transforming power and presence in our lives.

How, then, does the power of the Gospel transform our idolatrous hearts? Through repentance and faith. Jesus' message was simple but life-changing: "Repent and believe the good news!" (Mark 1:15). The Apostle Paul made clear that repentance and faith were to be ongoing in the life of the believer when he wrote, ". . . just as you received Christ Jesus as Lord, so walk in Him" (Colossians 2:6).

Through repentance, we pull our heart affections away from our idols and, by faith, put them back on Jesus Christ. We must all learn to ask, "What idol does my heart presently crave?" Once identified, we must be willing to take radical action against our idols, sapping their life-dominating power.

Repentance, however, is only half of our responsibility in transformation—the negative, defensive side of the equation. The other responsibility given to us in Scripture is the positive, offensive strategy called faith, which involves learning how to set the affections of our mind and heart on Christ. He wants us to enjoy Him and desire Him more than all of our idols.

Faith requires a continual rehearsing of and delighting in the many privileges that are now ours in Christ.

You are forgiven! Instead of continually punishing yourself for your sins, trying to earn forgiveness, or attempting to measure up to perfectionistic standards, you must learn to claim by faith God's promise of His eternal forgiveness through Christ's blood (Colossians 2:13). The Good News is that you can do absolutely nothing to make God love you any more or less! Thinking that your behavior causes you to phase in and out of His favor will short circuit your growth in grace.

You are accepted (2 Corinthians 5:21). You no longer need to fear rejection. You no longer must win the approval of others or hide your weaknesses. You don't always have to defend or build your reputation. You can stop trying to be who you are not and admit to God and others that you are a sinner. Now you can move toward others with a bold, Christ-like love—without fear of rejection.

You are adopted (1 John 3:1–2). You don't need to live or feel like a spiritual orphan anymore. God does not see you as merely a pardoned criminal, but as His very own son or daughter! You now have immediate access into the Father's presence, the promise of His provision for your every need, and the privilege of His discipline for your good.

You are free! No matter how defeated you may now feel in your battle with sin, you are no longer in bondage to it (Romans 6:5–18). No matter what your current struggle, true hope exists for lasting change.

You are not alone! Through faith in Christ you have been given the gift of the Holy Spirit to come alongside you, to comfort you, to encourage you and to empower you to live the life God has called you to live (John 16:5–15).

It has been said that a stone lying in the sun can't help but grow warm. In the same way, as we learn to expose our stony hearts to the warmth and light of the Gospel, we can't help but be transformed. We should preach this Good News to ourselves and others constantly, so that no matter what our struggles and fears may be, we can be encouraged, strengthened, and changed by hearing God's voice repeating these eternal truths to our hearts again and again.

All God asks is that we continue to draw near to Him in repentance and faith through the cross of Jesus Christ. It is here that we humble ourselves, cast away all our pride and self-sufficiency, and admit what we really are to God. It is here that we find the supernatural power, courage, and strength to be more like Jesus Christ.

Check off the assignments you've completed:

☐ Listened to Message 13

☐ Memorized Hebrews 9:14

☐ Completed the exercises

☐ Read "The Transforming Power of the Gospel"

☐ Updated your prayer partner

14 LIFESTYLE FORGIVENESS

The cross changes us. Pray to be awakened to the immensity of the love and forgiveness of our Father in relation to the people you're having trouble forgiving. Pray that he would show you the size of your debt, how much he loves you, and how much he's forgiven you. Out of that forgiveness, you'll find the power to forgive others.

GOALS:

- To experience the liberating joy that comes from realizing what a huge debt we have been forgiven
- To realize that the instinctive reaction of our hearts is to withhold forgiveness
- To see how the gospel empowers us to cancel the debts others owe us

>>> LISTEN TO MESSAGE 14

MESSAGE OUTLINE

1. Introduction: two illustrations

2. Lessons from the parable of the unmerciful servant (Matthew 18:23–35)

    a. Jesus is serious about forgiveness.

    b. Whatever you place your hope in is what you'll be judged by.

  c. A different path: receive mercy and grace from the King, and pass it on to others

  d. Peter's question

3. Our knee-jerk reaction to seek vengeance

  a. The rabbi's answer

  b. Lamech's song

4. Where will you get the power to forgive?

5. Our desperate need for the gospel

   a. The gospel means closing the bookkeeping department of your heart.

   b. Nobody outforgives the big-hearted king. You are forgiven much.

   c. Forgiveness is costly and requires death.

d. When we do not forgive, our hearts demand payment.

e. The sin against you is paltry in comparison to what you have been forgiven.

f. When you are unforgiving, you are disconnecting from Jesus and others. What now?
    • Connect to the gospel; pray to be awakened

    • Add to your debt

- Receive the King's love

- Hear God's forgiveness more than your sin

HOMEWORK

Name: Due:

Memorize:

Take words with you and return to the LORD. Say to him:
"Forgive all our sins and receive us graciously, that we may
offer the fruit of our lips."

—*Hosea 14:2*

Complete the following questions and exercises:

1. Review the list below:

Twenty gospel principles relating to forgiveness:
   1. My huge debt is canceled; I am released from God's wrath.
   2. Even my sins of unforgiveness are forgiven, covered, and
       forgotten.

3. Jesus has borne the anger and justice of God on my behalf, and continually intercedes for me.

4. The righteousness of Jesus' obedience (in loving and forgiving others perfectly) is credited to me.

5. I am neither a slave nor an orphan, alone and powerless.

6. I am now an heir, and a co-heir with Christ.

7. I have a compassionate High Priest who understands the trials and temptations I face as I struggle to forgive. He is there for me.

8. The Spirit of sonship lives within me, reminding me of my identity, guiding me to be like my Father, coming alongside me as my helper, and crying out on my behalf.

9. There is no condemnation directed against me, and no one can accuse me. I need not be afraid of seeing my lack of forgiveness toward others.

10. No one (and nothing) can separate me from my Father's love. He has already seen and paid for every dark part of my heart. Repentance can lead me to joy.

11. My Father is committed to my maturity and pursues me patiently and tirelessly toward that end. He has a glorious vision for me. I need not fear anything he wants to create in me.

12. I have not been given a spirit of fear or timidity. My Father fights for me, and has placed his courageous heart within me.

13. I have access to the throne of grace, and may boldly approach my Father with my struggle to forgive.

14. My heart has been sprinkled to cleanse me from a guilty conscience. I am set free from the bondage of guilt.

15. I have been set free from bondage to the "law" of forgiveness, and can earnestly seek to fulfill it as the expression of my Father's heart, in whom I delight.

16. Jesus is my holiness and sanctification. He is the author and the completer of what he has begun in me. I will finish the race.

17. I have been set free from bondage to Satan. My Father is victorious over him. I need not fear.

18. I have been set free from bondage to sin. My Father empowers me to follow his will in forgiving others.
19. My Father has made me a partner in his kingdom business. Forgiveness blows a hole in the gates of hell!
20. One day I will be made a perfect forgiver and lover like my Father, and will fellowship with him forever. He wants me to taste and enjoy more of this reality here and now.

Think of two people you still need to forgive (or forgive more deeply). You may want to choose a relationship you've already focused on earlier in the course. If you have trouble thinking of someone, consider times you've been hurt; people you've distanced yourself from in some way; people you no longer enjoy being around; people who stir up bad fruit—such as anger, gossip, a critical spirit; or an absence of kindness—whenever you see, hear, or think of them. Consider people with whom you've had relational conflicts—conflicts you still find yourself rehashing in your mind.

2. Write down your two choices (use initials and not real or full names).

    Person 1:

    Person 2:

3. What irritates or disturbs you most about these two people?

    Person 1:

    Person 2:

4. What are the "justice" issues here? How do you feel they've wronged you, hurt you, and sinned against you?

    Person 1:

    Person 2:

5. What conditions do you instinctively want to place on them before you truly forgive? In other words, what does your heart want to require from them before you release them? What specifically would you desire them to say or do?

   Person 1:

   Person 2:

6. How have you acted as a bookkeeper and kept a record of their wrongs? Where is there an accumulation of debt?

   Person 1:

   Person 2:

7. What are your knee-jerk reactions to these two people? How have you figuratively "choked" them and sought pay-ups and pay-backs? (Distancing ourselves from people would be one way of "choking" them.)

    Person 1:

    Person 2:

8. Seek to face the extent of the sin and loss involved, and the injury God is calling you to bear. Are you aware of ways you've sought to avoid or discount this? Have you grieved over this loss? It might be helpful to give yourself a day to fully meditate on this question, before moving on to question 9.

9. What additional aspects of injury and the debt owed to you would God want you to acknowledge?

10. Describe your own debt before God, and how it is far greater than the debt of Persons 1 and 2—and yet is canceled and forgiven. Do not rush through this question; take time to describe specifically your indebtedness.

11. Consider how the very things you hold against Persons 1 and 2 are also in you. What is the big log in your eye, compared to the speck in theirs (Luke 6:41–42)?

For example, John had trouble forgiving Andy, a rather pretentious know-it-all who left him feeling disrespected. One day, God showed John that although he was not showy, he was essentially guilty of the same attitude. John was a know-it-all about Andy's "know-it-allness"! Similarly, in the lecture, the speaker recounts that although he did not abuse others in the same way his abuser did, God showed him that his own lust and using of people were, at their core, the same thing.

12. How has your previous way of relating to these people reflected a small view of your own debt and a small view of Christ's forgiveness?

13. Describe your sin in not loving and forgiving Persons 1 and 2.

Person 1:

Person 2:

The gospel means that the debts which you are incapable of dealing with out of your own meager resources are well within the resources of your big-hearted Father. You have all you need in him to become more and more a radically forgiving son or daughter! Max Lucado tells the story of Daniel, a man who had long dreamed of owning his own gym. When he went to the bank to pick up the financing check, however, he discovered his brother had managed to use it to retire the mortgage on his own house. Daniel, a big man who had won ribbons for body-building, promised to break his brother's neck if he ever saw him again. Lucado describes their next encounter:

> The encounter occurred one day on a busy avenue. Let Daniel tell you in his own words what happened:
>
> I saw him, but he didn't see me. I felt my fists clench and my face get hot. My initial impulse was to grab him around the throat and choke the life out of him.
>
> But as I looked into his face, my anger began to melt. For as I saw him, I saw the image of my father. I saw my father's eyes. I saw my father's look. I saw my father's expression.

And as I saw my father in his face, my enemy once again became my brother.

Daniel walked toward him. The brother stopped, turned, and started to run, but he was too slow. Daniel reached out and grabbed his shoulder. The brother winced, expecting the worst. But rather than have his throat squeezed by Daniel's hands, he found himself hugged by Daniel's big arms. And the two brothers stood in the middle of the river of people and wept.

Daniel's words are worth repeating: "When I saw the image of my father in his face, my enemy became my brother."

Seeing the father's image in the face of the enemy. Try that. The next time you see or think of the one who broke your heart, look twice. As you look at his face, look also for His face—the face of the One who forgave you. Look into the eyes of the King who wept when you pleaded for mercy. Look into the face of the Father who gave you grace when no one else gave you a chance. Find the face of the God who forgives in the face of your enemy. And then, because God has forgiven you more than you'll ever be called on to forgive in another, set your enemy—and yourself—free.

And allow the hole in your heart to heal.

—Max Lucado, *The Applause of Heaven*,
pages 106–7

14. Explain how the gospel can now enable you to have compassion and genuine love toward these two people.

15. Describe some specific steps of love you will now take in these two relationships. Begin to pray for them and bless them. Be open to God's leading you to shower them with kindness and love. Update your prayer partner after you finish this question.

    Person 1:

    Person 2:

READ

Feeding Your Enemy

—Dan Allender, "Feeding Your Enemy," *Discipleship Journal*, 1992

Two unforgiving people sat in my office, defiant and afraid. Their lives had just been shattered. Janet had discovered a few days before that her husband, Gary, was involved in an affair with his secretary. The painful revelation had magnified their differences and deepened the chasm between them. Now, it seemed the only thing they had in common was the inability to forgive. Janet admitted with clipped irritation: "I know I should forgive him, but I can't do it." Gary quietly murmured, "I just can't forgive myself for the pain I have caused my family." The relationship seemed doomed.

Every day we face both transgressions that cry for forgiveness and God's unrelenting demand to forgive. Most of us struggle to forgive those who harm us. And the greater the damage, the more difficult it is to forgive. We often feel confused about what it means to forgive: "Should I just ignore the affair and somehow live as if it didn't happen?"

Other times we feel helpless to forgive those who have exacted a pound of flesh at our expense: "I've tried, but I just can't get rid of my bitterness." Our confusion is natural. God's relentless demand to forgive, to turn the other cheek, to offer one's coat to an enemy is at times infuriating, at other times seems illogical, and is always costly. No wonder the requirement to forgive is often seen as noble but impractical, or, just as tragically, applied without wisdom or understanding.

Forgiving others is not an easy concept to understand, let alone to apply. But there is not a more important subject in the Christian life. Let us then explore (I wish I could say answer) the question, What does it mean to love my enemy: the one who sexually abused me; my angry and insensitive spouse; my friend who gossiped behind my back and damaged my reputation; or even my child who snarls at my offer to go for a walk?

What is forgiveness?

Perhaps the best place to start in understanding what forgiveness is all about is to look at the way God forgives. God's forgiveness of us is a passionate movement of strength and mercy toward us, the offenders.

His bold strength is the force of His holiness, which will not rest until all sin is destroyed and His glory shines as the sun. His bold mercy constantly beckons us to return to His embrace, a place of rest and joy. He forgives our sin, but strongly moves to destroy the cancer within us that limits our joy and vitality; simultaneously, He extends arms of mercy to receive us as we turn back to Him. He fully faces the damage we have done while offering us a taste of kindness intended to lead us to repentance and reconciliation.

In the parable of the unmerciful servant, Jesus uses a dramatic picture to portray this kind of forgiveness: A master mercifully cancels an incomprehensible debt, freeing the debtor from imprisonment, shame, and destitution. The only debt that remains is to offer others a taste of redemptive love (Matthew 6:12–15; 18:21–35). Let me state a working definition of forgiveness, based on the scriptural picture of God's forgiveness. *To forgive another means to cancel a debt in order to provide a door of opportunity for (1) repentance and (2) restoration of the broken relationship.*

But understanding what forgiveness means and finding the strength within ourselves to offer it are two different matters. How can we get beyond an intellectual understanding and learn to forgive in the way God does? First, we need to get a glimpse of the frightening, surprising wonder of having been forgiven.

A forgiving heart knows how much it has been forgiven.

After Janet discovered her husband's affair, she became cold and indifferent toward him. Her energy was directed to survival. She could not bear (or so it seemed) to allow herself to feel the passion and tenderness required to forgive because her heart ached so deeply. But although she intended to remain aloof and superior, her occasional outbursts of punitive rage mocked her efforts.

The only prospect of forgiving Gary came when she realized divorce was the only other option. She was trapped between rage and reality. Rage allowed her to detach and survive; reality called her to an awareness that she did not want to raise her children, support herself, or face life alone. Forgiveness seemed like the only way back to a normal life, but forgiveness also seemed like a door that would open her heart to death.

Janet's desire for a return to normalcy was not strong enough to provide the energy to forgive. Assume for the moment that she is a Christian and knows something about God's forgiveness. What will it take for her to offer true forgiveness to Gary, a forgiveness that goes beyond pragmatic concerns?

When Jesus told His disciples that He expected them to forgive someone who hurt them time and time again, they knew instinctively that they didn't have the strength to obey. "Increase our faith!" was their reply to his admonition to forgive "seventy times seven times. He then promised: "If you have faith as small as a mustard seed, you can say to this mulberry tree, 'Be uprooted and planted in the sea,' and it will obey you" (Luke 17:3–6). What does faith have to do with forgiveness? What did the Lord mean when He said that even puny faith is sufficient to forgive again and again and again? Let me add one more thought before we tackle this question.

A forgiving heart offers to others a glimpse of the mysterious wonder of God's character. The energy to serve others a taste of God will be no greater than our own taste of God's forgiveness. Jesus said to an arrogant legalist, Simon, the Pharisee: "He who has been forgiven little loves little" (Luke 7:47). Jesus seems to be saying that the energy to forgive is directly related to our awareness of how much we have been forgiven, of how deeply we deserve God's condemnation. Simon was impressed with his own command of godliness; consequently, he was not drawn to the One who can forgive sin. The same is essentially true for us. What kind of faith, then, energizes both our ability to receive and offer forgiveness?

A true view of ourselves. Faith, even if it is as small as a mustard seed, makes us "certain of what we do *not* see" (Hebrews 11:1, emphasis added). The truth is that I am far worse than I appear; I am far worse than I even know. I need faith to see my own sin because my deceit makes me compare my sin with that of others and blinds me to my own need for forgiveness. Faith occasionally enables me to glimpse the depths of why I need God's ongoing mercy.

A true view of God. I also need faith to face the most incomprehensible fact: His glory moves toward me at the depths of my greatest rage against Him. He moves toward me with searing kindness and strong, open arms; with eyes that weep with delight at my return. Through faith I see beyond the veil of my presumption of innocence and into the heart of the Father who forgives sin.

Once we have experienced God's mercy and forgiveness, we will find the energy to cancel others' debts. A glimpse of His mercy quickens my faltering steps to offer to others a taste of it. And we will not stop with offering forgiveness, but, following God's example, we will pursue the one who hurt us for the purpose of reconciliation.

A forgiving heart yearns for reconciliation.

The driving passion of a forgiving heart is the desire to see, touch, taste, feel, and smell reconciliation. Most of us have experienced moments of tension with a friend. Though nothing is said, the air is heavy with an unknown, unstated offense. A forgiving heart seeks the kind of rest and joy we experience when the air is finally cleared and hearts are reconnected. Reconciliation is restored peace, true shalom, wholeness and health returned to something that was broken and diseased.

Reconciliation is costly for both the one offended and the offender. The offended forgives (cancels) the debt by not terminating the relationship, as might be reasonable and expected given the offense. Instead, he offers mercy and strength in order to restore the relationship. The cost for the offended is in withholding judgment and instead offering the possibility of restoration.

The cost for the offender is repentance. Reconciliation is never one-sided. (I forgive you and then you go scot-free, enabled to do harm again and again without any consequence.) Instead, forgiveness is an offer, but not the granting, of reconciliation.

Jesus said: "If your brother sins, rebuke him, and if he repents, forgive him. If he sins against you seven times in a day, and seven times comes back to you and says, 'I repent,' forgive him" (Luke 17:3–4). Is Jesus saying that forgiveness is conditional? That we are not to forgive unless the offender repents?

If that was His meaning, it would contradict His other teaching on forgiveness (see Matthew 6:12, 14–15; Mark 11:25; Luke 6:37). Clearly, we are to forgive, irrespective of the other person's response. What I believe He meant in the Luke 17 passage was that we are not to grant *reconciliation* until the person repents.

We see a picture of this principle in Jesus' cry from the Cross, "Father, forgive them." When the Lord forgave those who crucified Him, did He grant to each of them, at that moment, a place of eternal intimacy with His Father? I don't think so. I believe He was freeing them from the immediate consequences of killing Him. They deserved the kind of judgment that occurred in the Old Testament when Israelites touched the Ark of the Covenant: instant death. Jesus forestalled their punishment in asking for them to be forgiven. But they would have had to respond in repentance and faith, as did the thief who was crucified beside Jesus, in order for God to grant reconciliation.

What can we learn here? We must always offer reconciliation when, in the face of a rebuke, the offender demonstrates repentance: deep, heart-changing acknowledgment of sin and a radical redirection of life. But we need not extend restoration and peace to someone who has not repented.

A forgiving heart cancels the debt but does not lend new money until repentance occurs. A forgiving heart opens the door to any who knock. But entry into the home, that is, the heart, does not occur until the muddy shoes and dirty coat have been taken off. The offender must repent if true intimacy and reconciliation are ever to take place. That means that cheap forgiveness—peace at any cost—is not true forgiveness.

It is the passionate desire for reconciliation that enables us to offer true forgiveness. Forgiveness that is offered without the deep desire for the offender to be restored to God, and to the one who was harmed, is at best antiseptic and mechanical. At worst, it is pharisaical self-righteousness. Forgiveness is far, far more than a business transaction; it is the sacrifice of a heartbroken father who weeps over the loss of his child and longs to see the child restored to life and love and goodness.

Further, a forgiving heart does not wait passively for repentance to occur. Instead, it offers the offender a taste of mercy and strength designed to expose and destroy sin.

A forgiving heart works to destroy sin.

A forgiving heart hates sin and longs for reconciliation. Therefore, it works to destroy sin and offers strong incentives to repent and return to relationship. It offers "good food" that exposes the sinner's emptiness and tantalizes him to return to the Father's fold.

Paul tells us to offer food and drink to our enemy: "In doing this, you will heap burning coals on his head. Do not be overcome by evil, but overcome evil with good" (Romans 12:20–21). The idea of heaping burning coals on a head is a mixed metaphor that seems to symbolize God's smoldering, hot justice (Psalm 140:9–10). Yet it is also a symbol of mercy: As a sign of favor, Bedouins gave hot coals to someone who was without fire. And it is a metaphor of shame—coals on one's head turn the face red.

What is the point of this complex metaphor? I understand it to mean that offering goodness has two effects. It conquers evil by surprising and shaming the sinner, and it invites the evildoer to pursue life.

Surprise disrupts the enemy's expectations. The enemy usually has an idea, even if it's vague and unconscious, about how his victim will respond to his sin. Having his attack greeted with kindness and strength throws his perspective into disarray and foils his plans. The more radical the kindness, the more likely that his response will crumble in uncertainty.

Shame is the gift of exposure—it gives the enemy an opportunity to look deep inside to see what rules his heart. The curtain lifts, and he sees himself as the wizard of a sham kingdom. In that sense, shame is a severe mercy.

Every time we give our enemy a gift of "good food" we expose his sin in the light of God's goodness. What does it mean to offer our enemy "good food"? Good food is any gift that simultaneously reveals both God's mercy and strength. What will that look like in practice? The answer will likely be different in every situation. Let me give a few examples.

You might handle an angry, shaming attack directed against you by flight ("I'm sorry: I'll try and do better") or fight ("How dare you question my motives! What is your problem?"). In either case, the shaming attack worked—it unnerved you and gained control over your heart. In contrast, a response of "good food" would opt for neither flight nor fight. One woman said to her angry, shaming husband: "Honey, when you speak to me so angrily, it reminds me of how strong I know you can be. But when you try to bully me, it makes you appear weak." Her response pierced his rage and invited him to interact in a strong, passionate, and tender manner. Her words were strong—she exposed his hideous rage; and tender—with passion and grace, she invited him to move toward her. Good food is neither bitter (strong without mercy) nor saccharine (tender without strength).

I know a woman who struggles with her negative next-door neighbor. Every time her neighbor visits she finds fault with something. For months my friend quietly endured the assaults. Finally, after much thought and prayer, she respectfully and kindly asked her, "Jane, you always seem to be struggling with some injustice. How do you deal with all the inner pain you must feel?" My friend's good food was redemptive curiosity that highlighted both the neighbor's negativism and her inner struggle.

An enemy faced with the surprise and shame that result from being offered good food will respond with either fury or stunned disbelief. In either case, change will occur—either repentance or greater evil. The repentant heart comes out of the woods, declares defeat, and asks for honorable terms of surrender. The hardened heart comes out of the woods and brandishes a sword, declaring a call to arms. Evil can then be addressed and fought directly.

We are to offer others a taste of the Cross, which is a demonstration of both wrath and mercy. It is both a warning (God hates sin) and an invitation (embrace God's goodness and come under the blood of protection). To offer forgiveness we must have the tenderness to show mercy and the strength to intrude into the cancerous arrogance of the heart, knowing that the sin, if left untreated, will destroy the sinner's heart.

Check off the assignments you've completed:
☐ Listened to Message 14

☐ Memorized Hosea 14:2

☐ Completed the exercises

☐ Read "Feeding Your Enemy"

☐ Updated your prayer partner

15

PEACEKEEPING OR PEACEMAKING?

We almost automatically assume that conflict is bad and peacekeeping is good. However, peace*keeping* and peace*making* are two different things. The peace*keeper* is someone who tries to avoid constructive conflict by withdrawing or attacking, and often ends up in deeper conflict. The peace*maker* takes into account that life always involves struggle, and that at the heart of this conflict is a "love offensive" in relationship to others.

GOALS:

- To understand the difference between peacekeeping and peace-making
- To learn how to engage in constructive conflict
- To recognize some causes of destructive conflict

>>> LISTEN TO MESSAGE 15

MESSAGE OUTLINE

1. What is constructive conflict?

    a. Desiring God's glory

    b. Mounting a "love offensive"

    c. Winning the person, rather than the argument

    d. Dealing openly with differences without judging attitudes

    e.   Dealing with issues, not personalities

    f.   Asking questions, rather than accusing

    g.   Rejection of gossip—going directly to people

2.   What causes destructive conflict?

    a.   Christian cannibalism/irritability

b. Being "right"

c. Unexamined character flaws—look within your strong convictions

3. Who is qualified to engage in constructive conflict?

4. An eternal perspective

HOMEWORK

Name: Due:

Memorize:

"How can you say to your brother, 'Brother, let me take the speck out of your eye,' when you yourself fail to see the plank in your own eye? You hypocrite, first take the plank out of your own eye, and then you will see clearly to remove the speck from your brother's eye."

—Luke 6:42

Go over the following section carefully before moving on to the exercises:

Just keeping the peace or making it?
Peacemaking requires a willingness to be truthful and honest, and to boldly pursue others for their reconciliation with God and ourselves. However, it is vital that our own hearts be right as we engage in conflict, regardless of how or even whether the other party responds. In order to have the right heart toward others, we need to be living a lifestyle of repentance and forgiveness. Forgiving those who have in some way hurt

or injured us prepares our hearts to move toward them with a selfless love that seeks their best interest above our own, and demonstrates laying down our life for them. Otherwise, we will be peacekeepers—prone to either attack or retreat from those who hurt us.

Peacekeepers use different strategies to accomplish their goal of self-protection or to pursue their commitment to avoiding conflict. The path can be more passive or more aggressive. Sometimes we "peace-keep" in a more passive way by retreating—avoiding, withdrawing, denying, or covering up. Other times, we behave more aggressively by subduing—controlling, fixing, shaming, intimidating, attacking, or squelching. We may run and hide from problems with a friend, or we may steamroll over her, but in either case we're not concerned about loving God or that person. We merely want to feel at peace with ourselves, not make a true peace or pursue genuine reconciliation. So, perhaps surprisingly, we can be peacekeepers in either aggressive or passive ways. However, both options—retreating and subduing—are unloving. In the end, we're concerned only about our own self-protection and righteousness.

Complete the following questions and exercises:

1. Identify a relationship where you've been peacekeeping. Write down your choice (use initials, not real or full names).

2. Describe the conflict you've had, or perhaps need to have, but have avoided.

3. Peacekeeping is a way of murdering people in our hearts, whether by starving them out by retreating, or suffocating them by subduing them. Have you been more of a retreater or subduer? Describe two incidents in the above relationship that illustrate this. How do these action display a withholding of love from that person?

4. Review the following summary of the differences between peace-keeping and peacemaking as they relate to the aspects in the left-hand column.

Aspect	Peacekeeping	Peacemaking
Heart foundation	Unbelief, self-righteousness	Repentant faith, forgiveness
Power source	The sinful nature, fear	The Holy Spirit
Commitment	To avoid constructive conflict	To pursue constructive conflict
Direction	To bully, deny, or avoid	To invite to something far better
Feeling	Life is safe, less painful	Life is challenging, less certain
Goal	Self-protection, "peace"	God's glory, other person's good
Result	Alienation, broken relationships	Reconciliation, healed relationships

©2012 World Harvest Mission

5. Apply the summary above, and describe how each of the following has been evident in your conflict.

Heart foundation: What particular forms of unbelief (idols) drive this conflict? For example, have you been self-righteous or unforgiving? If so, in what ways?

Power source: What particular fears do you have that add fuel to this conflict?

Commitment: How have you avoided constructive conflict and genuine peacemaking?

Direction: Regarding this conflict, what are you angry about? What tactics have you used that demonstrate this anger?

Feeling and goal: How has this way of relating kept you safe, protected, and invulnerable?

Result: Describe the end result. What does this relationship currently look like?

6. Write a prayer of confession and repentance. Include any pride, unbelief, selfishness, harshness, or anger you've become conscious of.

7. Read the following actions and attitudes of someone engaged in constructive conflict. Take time to think over each item. Check the box below after you've done this.

    A person engaged in constructive conflict:

    ☐ Is more interested in winning the person than the argument.

    ☐ Deals humbly with differences without judging and condemning attitudes.

    ☐ Deals with issues, not personalities.

    ☐ Asks questions rather than accuses.

    ☐ Is approachable and teachable.

    ☐ Listens well. Desires the other person's good.

    ☐ Isn't interested in establishing how right he is and how wrong the other is.

    ☐ Expects God to use other people to expose her own need for the gospel.

    ☐ Does not exhibit a demanding attitude. Looks to the Holy Spirit to transform other people.

    ☐ Rejects gossip and deals directly with the person(s) involved.

    ☐ Prays for wisdom and grace, avoiding presumption about knowing what's best or right.

    ☐ Acknowledges self-deception and looks for his own log before looking for specks in others.

    ☐ Realizes that her strong convictions are often infected with sinful attitudes.

    ☐ Is committed to building mutual understanding.

    ☐ Is continually inviting people to something far better than they presently experience. Has a vision for what people can become.

    ☐ Desires that God's glory be seen in the lives of all people involved.

    ☐ Is committed to ongoing forgiveness, including during the course of further conversations.

8. What actions and attitudes from the list above have been missing in your relationship?

9. What elements of peacemaking are already present in your relationship?

10. Considering again the conflict you've been working through, describe below the lies you've tended to believe—and the opposing truth of the gospel.

    Lies about the other person [For example: They are the bigger sinner; God can't change them; they don't deserve compassion; they're hopeless; they'll never change.]

The truth about the other person [For example: They're just as needy as I am; God is concerned about them; God can change them.]

Lies about yourself [For example: I can't love them; I must protect myself at all costs; I have to change them; I must keep the peace.]

The truth about yourself [For example: God's Spirit can empower me to love this person; I don't have to change them.]

11. What might be the first steps of a "love offensive" toward this person?

12. How might God want you to move unselfishly toward them with a vision for his glory and what *he* can make them? Include specific and practical things that might be done or changed in your ways of relating to this person.

READ
Examine Yourself
—Ken Sande, *The Peacemaker*, pages 79–81, 87–90

Self-examination is especially important when we are involved in a dispute. Until we have dealt with our faults, it will be difficult to help others see how they have contributed to a dispute. But once we have confessed our wrongs and repaired any damage we have done, others will often be encouraged to follow our example and listen to our words. Here are some of the steps we can take to begin this process.

Be Honest About Sin

After five years of marriage, I can think of only one time I may have been entirely innocent of wrongdoing when Corlette and I had an argument (and I am probably mistaken about that incident). Every other time we have experienced a conflict, I either caused it or made it worse through sinful words or actions. Of course, when I am embroiled in the heat of battle, the last thing I naturally think about is my sin. But after the smoke clears, I can always see something that I should have done differently. With God's help, I am trying to speed up this process so I can avoid sinful reactions more often, or at least face up to them more quickly. . . .

Because most of us do not like to admit that we have sinned, we tend to conceal, deny, or rationalize our wrongs. If we cannot completely cover up what we have done, we try to minimize our wrongdoing by saying that we simply made a "mistake" or an "error in judgment." Another way to avoid responsibility for our sins is to shift the blame to others or to say that they made us act the way we did. When our wrongs are too obvious to ignore, it is easy to practice what I call the 40/60 Rule. It goes something like this: "Well, I know I'm not perfect, and I admit I am partially to blame for this problem. I'd say that about 40% of the fault is mine. That means 60% of the fault is hers. Since she is 20% more to blame than I am, she should be the one to ask for forgiveness." I never actually say or think these exact words, but I sometimes catch myself using this general concept in subtle ways. By believing that my sins have been more than cancelled by another's sins, I can divert attention from what I have done and avoid the call to repentance and confession. "If there is any confessing that needs to be done," I convince myself, "it needs to start with her."

Of course, we are only kidding ourselves when we try to cover up our sins. As I John 1:8 indicates, "If we claim to be without sin, we deceive ourselves and the truth is not in us" (cf. Psalm 36:2). Whenever we refuse to face up to our sins, we will eventually pay an unpleasant price. This is what King David discovered when he did not immediately repent of his sins. Psalm 32:3–5 describes the guilty conscience, emotional turmoil, and even the physical side effects that he experienced until he confessed his sins to God: "When I kept silent, my bones wasted away through my groaning all day long. For day and night your hand was heavy upon me; my strength was sapped as in the heat of summer. Then I acknowledged my sin to you and did not cover up my iniquity. I said, 'I will confess my sins to the Lord'—and you forgave the guilt of my sin."

Clearly, ignoring sin never pays. If it is difficult for you to identify and confess your wrongs, there are two things you can do. First, you can ask God to help you to see your sin clearly and repent of it, regardless of what others may do. As David prayed, "Search me, O God, and know my heart; test me and know my anxious thoughts. See if there is any offensive way in me, and lead me in the way everlasting" (Psalm 139:23–24). One of the ways that God will help you to see your sin is through the study of his Word. As you spend time in the Bible, learning what God has to say about the issues you face and the things you have done, you will often see where you have fallen short of his standards.

Second, it is often helpful to ask for the candid insights and advice of a spiritually mature friend (Proverbs 12:15; 19:20). This proved to be of real benefit to me one day after a woman called to confront me about a statement I had made about a mutual acquaintance. Although I "won" the discussion we had on the telephone (at least I thought so), my conscience bothered me afterward. Therefore, I described the situation to a friend and asked for his advice. Fortunately, Terry loved me enough to tell me the truth. He asked a few questions to clarify the situation and to unearth some facts I had conveniently passed over. Then he gently but firmly said that he thought I was wrong.

That was not what I wanted to hear, but when Terry explained his reasoning, I knew he was right. Five minutes later, after God helped me to overcome my pride, I called the woman back and admitted I was wrong. She graciously thanked me for my confession and freely forgave me. As I hung up the phone, I realized once more how much freedom we can experience if only we will deal with sin in God's way: "He who conceals his sins does not prosper, but whoever confesses and renounces them finds mercy" (Proverbs 28:13). . . .

Acknowledge Wrongful Motives

In James 4:1–3 we learn that the sinful words and actions common to conflict are merely symptoms of deeper problems: "What causes fights and quarrels among you? Don't they come from your desires that battle within you? You want something but don't get it. You kill and covet, but you cannot have what you want. You quarrel and fight. You do not have, because you do not ask God. When you do ask, you do not receive, because you ask with wrong motives, that you may spend what you get on your pleasures."

As James warns, it is not good enough to identify and repent of sinful words and actions. To maintain peace and make needed changes, you must also deal with the attitudes, desires, and motives that prompt you to do what you do. Jesus taught that sinful thoughts, words, and actions come "out of the heart" (Matthew 15:19; cf. Romans 1:24). In fact, he compared the heart to a tree that produces fruit (Luke 6:43–45). He explained that good behavior comes out of a good heart, and sinful behavior comes out of a bad heart (Luke 8:11–15; cf. Proverbs 4:23). Therefore, to achieve lasting changes in the way we live, real change must first occur in our hearts (see Ephesians 4:22–24).

The word *heart* is used in the Bible to describe more than just feelings. It often refers to our whole inner life, including thoughts and attitudes (Hebrews 4:12). Thus, when the Bible talks about changing our heart, it is calling for changes in feelings, desires, beliefs, expectations, thoughts, and attitudes. A supernatural transformation of your heart takes place when you accept Christ as your Savior, and then God works in you to continue the process of change. God promises: "I will cleanse you from all your impurities and from all your idols. I will give you a new heart and put a new spirit in you; I will remove from you your heart of stone and give you a heart of flesh" (Ezekiel 36:25b-26; cf. Hebrews 8:10).

As the above passage indicates, one aspect of getting a new heart is to be cleansed of our idols. An idol is not simply a statue of wood, stone, or metal; it is anything we love and pursue in place of God (see Philippians 3:19), and can also be referred to as a "false god" or a "functional god." In biblical terms, an idol is something other than God that we set our hearts on (Luke 12:29; 1 Corinthians 10:6), that motivates us (1 Corinthians 4:5), that masters or rules us (Psalm 119:133), or that we serve (Matthew 6:24).

Even genuine Christians struggle with idolatry. Although we believe in God and say we want to serve him only, at times we allow other influences to master us. We allow our lives to revolve around the deceitful desires of our hearts rather than around God and his revealed purposes. Listed below are a few of the idols, or functional gods, that slip into our lives, draw us away from the Lord, and contribute to conflict.

1. Improper desires for physical pleasure—lusts of the flesh (1 John 2:15–17; cf. Galatians 5:16–21; Ephesians 4:19). This kind of idol is often characterized by an aversion to disciplining one's mind, spirit, or body. Lusts of the flesh can include sexual unfaithfulness, gambling, overeating, or the abuse of drugs or alcohol, which in turn can cause marital or employment problems. The pursuit of pleasure can also lead to laziness, which often results in financial distress.

2. Pride and arrogance. It is also idolatrous to be preoccupied with one's own wisdom, accomplishments, power, abilities, reputation, or possessions (Proverbs 8:13; 2 Corinthians 5:12; James 3:14; 1 John 2:15–17). Pride can make us reluctant to admit our wrongs, which leads to excessive defensiveness and an obsession with self-justification. It can also cause us to dominate discussions or insist on getting our own way because we believe we know all the answers. Proud people are often reluctant to seek or listen to the counsel of others and may even resent offered advice. This can contribute to unwise decisions and a tendency to blame others for problems that arise.

3. Love of money (or other material possessions) (1 Timothy 6:10). Greed is specifically referred to as idolatry (Ephesians 5:5). This kind of false god can also appear as envy, an excessive desire for financial security, boasting about what we possess, or an unhealthy delight in possessing something (Matthew 6:24; Luke 12:16–21; 27–31; Acts 5:1–3). "Love of money" can cause us to lie, break contracts, do shoddy work, mistreat employees, violate copyright laws, or compulsively pursue unnecessary things. It can also make it difficult to forgive debts or show mercy.

4. Fear of man. This can take many forms. Sometimes it involves an actual fear of what others can do to us (Proverbs 29:25; Luke 12:4–5), but it is most commonly seen as an excessive concern about what others think about us. This can lead to a preoccupation with acceptance, approval, popularity, personal comparisons, self- image, or pleasing others (John 9:22; 12:42–43; Galatians 1:10; 1 Thessalonians 2:4). This idol can make us reluctant to confront serious sin. The constant desire for approval and acceptance can cause us to gossip or keep us from speaking out on moral issues. It can also make us do things we really know are not right, eventually leading to guilt and resentment. Furthermore, if we fear what others may think of us, we may also be reluctant to admit our wrongs or ask for help, which often prolongs conflict.

5. Good things that we want too much. These most subtle idols include love, happiness, good health, companionship, children, success, prosperity, recreation, goodwill, influence, status, a good image, or even spiritual power (Luke 12:27–34). These things, while beneficial in themselves, can become idols if we want them for the wrong reasons, if our thoughts and actions revolve around them, or if our failure to have them is a major source of discontent. An obsessive longing for love and happiness can lead to an abandonment of family and professional commitments. Conversely, the desire for a notable reputation can result in workaholism, a prime contributor to marital disputes.

Idols—the things of the world—can motivate or master us. They influence what we think about, where we invest our time, how we handle our rights and resources, and how we deal with other people. Many of these idols are hard to identify because their influence is sporadic. We may follow God faithfully most of the day, and then, when momentarily faced with a single decision, we may serve an idol rather than God. This is especially true when we are involved in conflict. Although we may have every intention of behaving in a godly way, when we actually come face to face with our opponent, we suddenly say and do things we never planned. This behavior often indicates that there are some idols we need to root out of our hearts.

Check off the assignments you've completed:
- ☐ Listened to Message 15
- ☐ Memorized Luke 6:42
- ☐ Completed the exercises
- ☐ Read "Examine Yourself"
- ☐ Updated your prayer partner

16 WEAKNESS EVANGELISM

If you say you love people but don't respect them, they won't understand what you're saying. When you begin communicating the gospel to others outside of your own group, you must see that the key is respecting people. With a childlike confidence in the Holy Spirit's presence, you're willing to be with those who are different from you. Humble your heart, and take risks. Go and die. Risk and you will never rust.

GOALS:

- To realize that our Father calls us into partnership in his exciting business of changing lives
- To recognize that we much prefer to "rust in peace" rather than "risk in faith"
- To understand how the gospel moves us out in ways that deepen our faith and bring glory to God

>>> LISTEN TO MESSAGE 16

MESSAGE OUTLINE

1. "Perfecting" people in our own image

2. How to win others for Christ

    a. Risk or rust

    b. Faith deepening during trip to Uganda

    c. Let God be God—let go of your idols

3. Changing from the inside

    a. Humility, and an upsetting, childlike simplicity

    b. Doing unto others

    c. Respecting people

    d. The presence of God through prayer.

4.   Push the envelope—go and die

5.   Look at who Jesus ministers to—not culturally bound

6.   An illustration: Jean Valjean

HOMEWORK

Name: Due:

Memorize:

"So in everything, do to others what you would have them
do to you, for this sums up the Law and the Prophets."
—Matthew 7:12

Complete the following questions and exercises:

1. Write a one-page testimony of what the Lord has done in your life
    since you began *Sonship*. Consider areas in your life and relation-
    ships that God has changed. What fears and offensive ways (Psalm
    139:23–24) have been exposed and impacted by the gospel? How
    have you changed in the way you relate to people—especially those
    close to you?

2. In what areas and ways do you want God to change you in the coming year?

Hebrews 3:12–13 reads, "See to it, brothers, that none of you has a sinful, unbelieving heart that turns away from the living God. But encourage one another daily, as long as it is called Today, so that none of you may be hardened by sin's deceitfulness." We all decay spiritually. In one day, we can be hardened by sin if we're not being encouraged to greater faith in Jesus. Like the Israelites of old, we cannot survive on yesterday's manna. So we need to be thinking of ways to keep the gospel message fresh for ourselves every day. One way is to keep telling others the story of what God is doing in our lives, using new illustrations of how the gospel and the Spirit are changing us. Another way, related to this, is to continue to invite other people's insights into our lives. For example, if your spouse says, "You seem a little irritated tonight," instead of responding (with irritation), "Well, I'm not!" you can live by repentance and faith and ask, "Why do you say that? Can you tell me more?" Or, if your kids make the observation, "Mom, you seem grumpy," you might ask them how your grumpiness makes them feel. Invite honest feedback from people who are close to you.

3. How will you keep the gospel message fresh for yourself?

4. How do you plan to minister to others? What sort of one-on-one relationships can you envision? What discipling relationships could you get into?

5. Name an unbeliever in your life whom you think God is calling you to pray for and share your life—and the gospel—with. What is your vision for this person? How could you see the glory of God revealed through him or her?

6. Consider all you've learned in this course about God's love and mercy toward you. How might this realization give you compassion for the person in question 5? Specifically mention at least two ways.

7. How might the golden rule, "So in everything, do to others what you would have them do to you, for this sums up the Law and the Prophets" (Matthew 7:12), direct or change your approach to this person?

8. The speaker states, "If you say you love people but do not respect them, they will not understand what you are saying." How can you pray for and demonstrate respect for this person?

9. This week's reading discusses doing evangelism from a position of weakness. What is the role of "your story" in evangelism? How might it influence your approach? How does it encourage you?

10. The speaker talks about how God used his praying for people to reach them. How might you offer to pray for this person? When? What other acts of kindness might you begin to show this person?

READ
Weakness Evangelism

Despite my tall and lanky frame, I'm not a basketball star. In fact, I never liked sports much at all. It might have something to do with poor coordination as a kid, being more artistically inclined, or perhaps I just missed the sports gene. In any case, it's difficult being an American male who doesn't know one team from the next. At times, it can limit conversation. I used to fake it—you know, pretend I really knew the sport when I didn't. Sometimes that worked out well, and I could get by until the subject changed. But other times it led to some awkward moments when my ignorance became apparent. Moreover, there was never any doubt about my ignorance when I attempted to play. For me the only thing worse than talking about sports was actually playing them. Why in the world would anyone choose to do something extremely poorly in public? It's like a soloist singing off-key—it's painful for everyone. Besides, I hate feeling incompetent.

Why do you suppose I faked it? What does believing the gospel look like in the midst of something you are not good at? Furthermore, could God use my inability for his glory? I used to think that God would work only through an area of my strength, such as my verbal ability. However, the older I get the more I realize that usually this is not the case.

My neighbor Winston (not his real name) is quite a character. He's the most idealistically kindhearted person I know. Politically, he's an extreme left-wing liberal.

He is tolerant, fun-loving, and not a little proud of how irreligious and irreverent he is. He loves to party and have a good time. He works hard as a psychiatric social worker, sticking up for the rights of those who need an advocate in the system. We're both fixing up our old cars and became friends by comparing ideas and helping each other out. One of the things that drew me to Winston was his idealism and his love of people. One of the things that drew him to me was my honesty about some of my struggles. In one of our first conversations, I told him how impatient I had been with my kids that day, and how Mr. Hyde had reared his ugly head, seemingly out of nowhere. He easily identified with me, and admitted his own weakness in this area.

One night I told Winston that I had just had a fight with my wife and that I was struggling with resentment toward her. He was surprised, saying he always figured we were a couple who just didn't fight. He went on to tell me about a fight he had had with his own wife that very day. I talked with him briefly about how conflict with my wife brings out my deep desire to be right. And when we both want to be right, we can never resolve anything because we only care about our own reputations—we're getting our sense of rightness at the expense of our spouse. Winston was curious, and I told him a little about how knowing that I'm right with God allows me the freedom to admit when I'm wrong and hurtful toward my wife.

So when Winston called me to go and play basketball with him and some of the other guys from the neighborhood, I knew it was another great opportunity to hang out with him as a friend. But internally I groaned—basketball, of all things! Why basketball? I said I would go, but told Winston that I was a lousy player. He assured me that he too was lousy and that none of the guys took it seriously. It was just an opportunity to blow off some steam and have fun.

One of the main things I've been learning in my spiritual journey is recognizing where my worth and value ultimately come from. I tend to derive my sense of value from the esteem of other people. This can create a lot of anxiety, because gaining and keeping the esteem of others is hard work. The gospel has been teaching me that worth, acceptance, and righteousness come from the Lord alone. All other attempts to generate worth are a false security, a form of idolatry, and are therefore doomed to fail. So some of the benefits of letting my weaknesses show have been a deeper honesty with people about who I am and a greater freedom to admit how deeply I need the Lord.

I knew that playing basketball was an opportunity to put into practice all the theology that I so dearly held to intellectually. If Jesus has justified me, and declared me fully acceptable to himself, then can I worry about looking like a fool on the basketball court? Before I heard the beep of Winston's horn, I asked my nine-year-old son to remind me which direction to run when I had the ball. That proved to be very helpful information! I was actually excited about playing. I ran up and down the court with almost as much enthusiasm as my uninhibited son. I had a lot of fun, and even held my own in defense. I missed every shot I took, dribbled when I should have held the ball, and shot when I should have dribbled, but the guys were patient with me.

I was having fun living by faith! However, when the time came to choose sides for the next game my heart sank. The team captains picked players, and it felt just like junior high: would I be the last one picked? When my name was called last I had a "shame attack." But even that was an opportunity to remind myself that the Lord loved me and was pleased with me. It didn't immobilize me as it might have done in the past. Don't get me wrong. I'd still like to be a great player and be picked first. However, I wasn't taking myself too seriously, which showed that the Lord was at work. I didn't experience a total freedom, but I did have a greater sense that even in my awkwardness, Jesus was my friend and he was proud of me. Afterwards, Winston and I ended up talking at his house.

The first thing he said to me was, "You really do suck at basketball, don't you?"

"You said you sucked too," I protested, "but you can actually play."

"No, I can't," he replied, "it's just that you're so bad that—next to you—I look like Magic Johnson!"

The most important thing about repenting and living by faith as a child of God is that dependence on God gives him glory and provides us an opportunity to experience closeness with him. But it also seems admitting our weakness before God and being willing to fail in front of people is an invitation to experience closeness with them. As Winston and I sat on his porch bantering back and forth I asked him, "Winston, what has motivated your social conscience?" That question led him to open up about his childhood. He told me his story and trusted me with a lot of risky information about himself. After about an hour he asked me a similar question, knowing that I too am concerned about improving people's lives. What resulted was an opportunity to share my story and the quest for righteousness that Jesus has fulfilled. I told him of my search for meaning and of my need for forgiveness. I told him about some of my "junk" as well. He was frank about not desiring God or thinking that God is necessary to live a good life. So I asked him if he ever felt the need to be forgiven. He thought about that for a long time and finally answered, "Yes." He admitted to struggling with guilt.

A year later, Winston is still not a believer, to my knowledge. We continue to have a good friendship. In fact, our friendship has grown and we respect each other a lot. I don't feel any pressure to convert him. But I do love him and pray earnestly for his salvation. We're honest with each other. Usually when we talk about the Lord it's when I have been honest about a struggle I'm having, or an area where I am weak in some way. My reputation doesn't matter as much to me as it used to. At one time, I was striving to give an answer to people like Winston, so that I would be "right." Now, I'm more inclined to ask the Holy Spirit to give me a question, so that I can know people better and meet them where they are, instead of where I would like them to be.

Check off the assignments you've completed:

☐ Listened to Message 16

☐ Memorized Matthew 7:12

☐ Completed the exercises

☐ Read "Weakness Evangelism"

☐ Updated your prayer partner

Appendix

A GALATIANS

INTRODUCTION

When men and women get their hands on religion, one of the first things they often do is turn it into an instrument for controlling others, either putting or keeping them "in their place." The history of such religious manipulation and coercion is long and tedious. It is little wonder that people who have only known religion on such terms experience release or escape from it as freedom. The problem is that the freedom turns out to be short-lived.

Paul of Tarsus was doing his diligent best to add yet another chapter to this dreary history when he was converted by Jesus to something radically and entirely different—a free life in God. Through Jesus, Paul learned that God was not an impersonal force to be used to make people behave in certain prescribed ways, but a personal Savior who set us free to live a free life. God did not coerce us from without, but set us free from within.

It was a glorious experience, and Paul set off telling others, introducing and inviting everyone he met into this free life. In his early travels he founded a series of churches in the Roman province of Galatia. A few years later Paul learned that religious leaders of the old school had come into those churches, called his views and authority into question, and were reintroducing the old ways, herding all these freedom-loving Christians back into the corral of religious rules and regulations.

Paul was, of course, furious. He was furious with the old guard for coming in with their strong-arm religious tactics and intimidating the

258

Christians into giving up their free life in Jesus. But he was also furious with the Christians for caving in to the intimidation.

His letter to the Galatian churches helps them, and us, recover the original freedom. It also gives direction in the nature of God's gift of freedom—most necessary guidance, for freedom is a delicate and subtle gift, easily perverted and often squandered.

THE BOOK OF GALATIANS
(The Message translation)

1 **I, Paul, and my companions** in faith here, send greetings to the Galatian churches. My authority for writing to you does not come from any popular vote of the people, nor does it come through the appointment of some human higher-up. It comes directly from Jesus the Messiah and God the Father, who raised him from the dead. I'm God-commissioned. So I greet you with the great words, grace and peace! We know the meaning of those words because Jesus Christ rescued us from this evil world we're in by offering himself as a sacrifice for our sins. God's plan is that we all experience that rescue. Glory to God forever! Oh, yes!

The Message

I can't believe your fickleness—how easily you have turned traitor to him who called you by the grace of Christ by embracing a variant message! It is not a minor variation, you know; it is completely other, an alien message, a no-message, a lie about God. Those who are provoking this agitation among you are turning the Message of Christ on its head. Let me be blunt: If one of us—even if an angel from heaven!—were to preach something other than what we preached originally, let him be cursed. I said it once; I'll say it again: If anyone, regardless of reputation or credentials, preaches something other than what you received originally, let him be cursed.

Do you think I speak this strongly in order to manipulate crowds? Or curry favor with God? Or get popular applause? If my goal was popularity, I wouldn't bother being Christ's slave. Know this—I am most emphatic here, friends—this great Message I delivered to you is not mere human optimism. I didn't receive it through the traditions, and I wasn't taught it in some school. I got it straight from God, received the Message directly from Jesus Christ.

I'm sure that you've heard the story of my earlier life when I lived in the Jewish way. In those days I went all out in persecuting God's church. I was systematically destroying it. I was so enthusiastic about the traditions of my ancestors that I advanced head and shoulders above my peers in my career. Even then God had designs on me. Why, when I was still in my mother's womb he chose and called me out of sheer generosity! Now he has intervened and revealed his Son to me so that I might joyfully tell non-Jews about him.

Immediately after my calling—without consulting anyone around me and without going up to Jerusalem to confer with those who were apostles long before I was—I got away to Arabia. Later I returned to Damascus, but it was three years before I went up to Jerusalem to compare stories with Peter. I was there only fifteen days—but what days they were! Except for our Master's brother James, I saw no other apostles. (I'm telling you the absolute truth in this.)

Then I began my ministry in the regions of Syria and Cilicia. After all that time and activity I was still unknown by face among the Christian churches in Judea. There was only this report: "That man who once persecuted us is now preaching the very message he used to try to destroy." Their response was to recognize and worship God because of me!

What Is Central?

2 **Fourteen years after that first visit,** Barnabas and I went up to Jerusalem and took Titus with us. I went to clarify with them what had been revealed to me. At that time I placed before them exactly what I was preaching to the non-Jews. I did this in private with the leaders, those held in esteem by the church, so that our concern would not become a controversial public issue, marred by ethnic tensions, exposing my years of work to denigration and endangering my present ministry. Significantly, Titus, non-Jewish though he was, was not required to be circumcised. While we were in conference we were infiltrated by spies pretending to be Christians, who slipped in to find out just how free true Christians are. Their ulterior motive was to reduce us to their brand of servitude. We didn't give them the time of day. We were determined to preserve the truth of the Message for you.

As for those who were considered important in the church, their reputation doesn't concern me. God isn't impressed with mere appearances, and neither am I. And of course these leaders were able to add nothing to the message I had been preaching. It was soon evident that God had entrusted me with the same message to the non-Jews as Peter had been preaching to the Jews. Recognizing that my calling had been given by God, James, Peter, and John—the pillars of the church—shook hands with me and Barnabas, assigning us to a ministry to the non-Jews, while they continued to be responsible for reaching out to the Jews. The only additional thing they asked was that we remember the poor, and I was already eager to do that.

Later, when Peter came to Antioch, I had a face-to-face confrontation with him because he was clearly out of line. Here's the situation. Earlier, before certain persons had come from James, Peter regularly ate with the non-Jews. But when that conservative group came from Jerusalem, he cautiously pulled back and put as much distance as he could manage between himself and his non-Jewish friends. That's how fearful he was of the conservative Jewish clique that's been pushing the old system of circumcision. Unfortunately, the rest of the Jews in the Antioch church joined in that hypocrisy so that even Barnabas was swept along in the charade.

But when I saw that they were not maintaining a steady, straight course according to the Message, I spoke up to Peter in front of them all: "If you, a Jew, live like a non-Jew when you're not being observed by the watchdogs from Jerusalem, what right do you have to require non-Jews to conform to Jewish customs just to make a favorable impression on your old Jerusalem cronies?"

We Jews know that we have no advantage of birth over "non-Jewish sinners." We know very well that we are not set right with God by rule keeping but only through personal faith in Jesus Christ. How do we know? We tried it—and we had the best system of rules the world has ever seen! Convinced that no human being can please God by self-improvement, we believed in Jesus as the Messiah so that we might be set right before God by trusting in the Messiah, not by trying to be good.

Have some of you noticed that we are not yet perfect? (No great surprise, right?) And are you ready to make the accusation that since people like me, who go through Christ in order to get things right with God, aren't perfectly virtuous, Christ must therefore be an accessory to sin? The accusation is frivolous. If I was "trying to be good," I would be rebuilding the same old barn that I tore down. I would be acting as a charlatan.

What actually took place is this: I tried keeping rules and working my head off to please God, and it didn't work. So I quit being a "law man" so that I could be God's man. Christ's life showed me how, and enabled me to do it. I identified myself completely with him. Indeed, I have been crucified with Christ. My ego is no longer central. It is no longer important that I appear righteous before you or have your good opinion, and I am no longer driven to impress God. Christ lives in me. The life you see me living is not "mine," but it is lived by faith in the Son of God, who loved me and gave himself for me. I am not going to go back on that.

Is it not clear to you that to go back to that old rule-keeping, peer-pleasing religion would be an abandonment of everything personal and free in my relationship with God? I refuse to do that, to repudiate God's grace. If a living relationship with God could come by rule keeping, then Christ died unnecessarily.

Trust in Christ, Not the Law

3 **You crazy Galatians!** Did someone put a hex on you? Have you taken leave of your senses? Something crazy has happened, for it's obvious that you no longer have the crucified Jesus in clear focus in your lives. His sacrifice on the Cross was certainly set before you clearly enough.

Let me put this question to you: How did your new life begin? Was it by working your heads off to please God? Or was it by responding to God's Message to you? Are you going to continue this craziness? For only crazy people would think they could complete by their own efforts what was begun by God. If you weren't smart enough or strong enough to begin it, how do you suppose you could perfect it? Did you go through this whole painful learning process for nothing? It is not yet a total loss, but it certainly will be if you keep this up!

Answer this question: Does the God who lavishly provides you with his own presence, his Holy Spirit, working things in your lives you could never do for yourselves, does he do these things because of your strenuous moral striving or because you trust him to do them in you? Don't these things happen among you just as they happened with Abraham? He believed God, and that act of belief was turned into a life that was right with God.

Is it not obvious to you that persons who put their trust in Christ (not persons who put their trust in the law!) are like Abraham: children of faith? It was all laid out beforehand in Scripture that God would set things right with non-Jews by faith. Scripture anticipated this in the promise to Abraham: "All nations will be blessed in you."

So those now who live by faith are blessed along with Abraham, who lived by faith—this is no new doctrine! And that means that anyone who tries to live by his own effort, independent of God, is doomed to failure. Scripture backs this up: "Utterly cursed is every person who fails to carry out every detail written in the Book of the law."

The obvious impossibility of carrying out such a moral program should make it plain that no one can sustain a relationship with God that way:

The person who lives in right relationship with God does it by embracing what God arranges for him. Doing things for God is the opposite of entering into what God does for you. Habakkuk had it right: "The person who believes God, is set right by God—and that's the real life." Rule keeping does not naturally evolve into living by faith, but only perpetuates itself in more and more rule keeping, a fact observed in Scripture: "The one who does these things [rule keeping continues to live by them."

Christ redeemed us from that self-defeating, cursed life by absorbing it completely into himself. Do you remember the Scripture that says, "Cursed is everyone who hangs on a tree"? That is what happened when Jesus was nailed to the Cross: He became a curse, and at the same time dissolved the curse. And now, because of that, the air is cleared and we can see that Abraham's blessing is present and available for non-Jews, too. We are all able to receive God's life, his Spirit, in and with us by believing—just the way Abraham received it.

Friends, let me give you an example from everyday affairs of the free life I am talking about. Once a person's will has been ratified, no one else can annul it or add to it. Now, the promises were made to Abraham and to his descendant. You will observe that Scripture, in the careful language of a legal document, does not say "to descendants," referring to everybody in general, but "to your descendant" (the noun, note, is singular), referring to Christ. This is the way I interpret this: A will, earlier ratified by God, is not annulled by an addendum attached 430 years later, thereby negating the promise of the will. No, this addendum, with its instructions and regulations, has nothing to do with the promised inheritance in the will.

What is the point, then, of the law, the attached addendum? It was a thoughtful addition to the original covenant promises made to Abraham. The purpose of the law was to keep a sinful people in the way of salvation until Christ (the descendant) came, inheriting the promises and distributing them to us. Obviously this law was not a firsthand encounter with God. It was arranged by angelic messengers through a middleman, Moses. But if there is a middleman as there was at Sinai, then the people are not dealing directly with God, are they? But the original promise is the direct blessing of God, received by faith.

If such is the case, is the law, then, an anti-promise, a negation of God's will for us? Not at all. Its purpose was to make obvious to everyone that we are, in ourselves, out of right relationship with God, and therefore to show us the futility of devising some religious system for getting by our own efforts what we can only get by waiting in faith for God to complete his promise. For if any kind of rule keeping had power to create life in us, we would certainly have gotten it by this time.

Until the time when we were mature enough to respond freely in faith to the living God, we were carefully surrounded and protected by the Mosaic law. The law was like those Greek tutors, with which you are familiar, who escort children to school and protect them from danger or distraction, making sure the children will really get to the place they set out for.

But now you have arrived at your destination: By faith in Christ you are in direct relationship with God. Your baptism in Christ was not just washing you up for a fresh start. It also involved dressing you in an adult faith wardrobe—Christ's life, the fulfillment of God's original promise.

In Christ's Family

In Christ's family there can be no division into Jew and non-Jew, slave and free, male and female. Among us you are all equal. That is, we are all in a common relationship with Jesus Christ. Also, since you are Christ's family; then you are Abraham's famous "descendant," heirs according to the covenant promises.

4 **Let me show you** the implications of this. As long as the heir is a minor, he has no advantage over the slave. Though legally he owns the entire inheritance, he is subject to tutors and administrators until whatever date the father has set for emancipation. That is the way it is with us: When we were minors, we were just like slaves ordered around

by simple instructions (the tutors and administrators of this world), with no say in the conduct of our own lives.

But when the time arrived that was set by God the Father, God sent his Son, born among us of a woman, born under the conditions of the law so that he might redeem those of us who have been kidnapped by the law. Thus we have been set free to experience our rightful heritage. You can tell for sure that you are now fully adopted as his own children because God sent the Spirit of his Son into our lives crying out, "Papa! Father!" Doesn't that privilege of intimate conversation with God make it plain that you are not a slave, but a child? And if you are a child, you're also an heir, with complete access to the inheritance.

Earlier, before you knew God personally, you were enslaved to so-called gods that had nothing of the divine about them. But now that you know the real God—or rather since God knows you—how can you possibly subject yourselves again to those paper tigers? For that is exactly what you do when you are intimidated into scrupulously observing all the traditions, taboos, and superstitions associated with special days and seasons and years. I am afraid that all my hard work among you has gone up in a puff of smoke!

My dear friends, what I would really like you to do is try to put yourselves in my shoes to the same extent that I, when I was with you, put myself in yours. You were very sensitive and kind then. You did not come down on me personally. You were well aware that the reason I ended up preaching to you was that I was physically broken, and so, prevented from continuing my journey, I was forced to stop with you. That is how I came to preach to you.

And don't you remember that even though taking in a sick guest was most troublesome for you, you chose to treat me as well as you would have treated an angel of God—as well as you would have treated Jesus himself if he had visited you? What has happened to the satisfaction you felt at that time? There were some of you then who, if possible, would have given your very eyes to me—that is how deeply you cared! And now have I suddenly become your enemy simply by telling you the truth? I can't believe it.

Those heretical teachers go to great lengths to flatter you, but their motives are rotten. They want to shut you out of the free world of God's grace so that you will always depend on them for approval and direction, making them feel important.

It is a good thing to be ardent in doing good, but not just when I am in your presence. Can't you continue the same concern for both my person and my message when I am away from you that you had when I was with you? Do you know how I feel right now, and will feel until Christ's life becomes visible in your lives? Like a mother in the pain of childbirth. Oh, I keep wishing that I was with you. Then I wouldn't be reduced to this blunt, letter-writing language out of sheer frustration.

Tell me now, you who have become so enamored with the law: Have you paid close attention to that law? Abraham, remember, had two sons: one by the slave woman and one by the free woman. The son of the slave woman was born by human connivance; the son of the free woman was born by God's promise. This illustrates the very thing we are dealing with now. The two births represent two ways of being in relationship with God. One is from Mount Sinai in Arabia. It corresponds with what is now going on in Jerusalem—a slave life, producing slaves as offspring. This is the way of Hagar. In contrast to that, there is an invisible Jerusalem, a free Jerusalem, and she is our mother—this is the way of Sarah. Remember what Isaiah wrote:

> Rejoice, barren woman who bears no children,
> shout and cry out, woman who has no birth pangs,
> Because the children of the barren woman
> now surpass the children of the chosen woman.

Isn't it clear, friends, that you, like Isaac, are children of promise? In the days of Hagar and Sarah, the child who came from faithless connivance (Ishmael) harassed the child who came—empowered by the Spirit—from the faithful promise (Isaac). Isn't it clear that the harassment you are now experiencing from the Jerusalem heretics follows that old pattern? There is a Scripture that tells us what to do: "Expel the slave mother with her son, for the slave son will not inherit with the free son." Isn't that conclusive? We are not children of the slave woman, but of the free woman.

The Life of Freedom

5 **Christ has set us free** to live a free life. So take your stand! Never again let anyone put a harness of slavery on you.

I am emphatic about this. The moment anyone of you submits to circumcision or any other rule-keeping system, at that same moment Christ's hard-won gift of freedom is squandered. I repeat my warning: The person who accepts the ways of circumcision trades all the advantages of the free life in Christ for the obligations of the slave life of the law.

I suspect you would never intend this, but this is what happens. When you attempt to live by your own religious plans and projects, you are cut off from Christ, you fall out of grace. Meanwhile we expectantly wait for a satisfying relationship with the Spirit. For in Christ, neither our most conscientious religion nor disregard of religion amounts to anything. What matters is something far more interior: faith expressed in love.

You were running superbly! Who cut in on you, deflecting you from the true course of obedience? This detour doesn't come from the One who called you into the race in the first place. And please don't toss this off as insignificant. It only takes a minute amount of yeast, you know, to permeate an entire loaf of bread. Deep down, the Master has given me confidence that you will not defect. But the one who is upsetting you, whoever he is, will bear the divine judgment.

As for the rumor that I continue to preach the ways of circumcision (as I did in those pre-Damascus Road days), that is absurd. Why would I still be persecuted, then? If I were preaching that old message, no one would be offended if I mentioned the Cross now and then—it would be so watered-down it wouldn't matter one way or the other. Why don't these agitators, obsessive as they are about circumcision, go all the way and castrate themselves!

It is absolutely clear that God has called you to a free life. Just make sure that you don't use this freedom as an excuse to do whatever you want to do and destroy your freedom. Rather, use your freedom to serve one another in love; that's how freedom grows. For everything we know about God's Word is summed up in a single sentence: Love others as you love yourself. That's an act of true freedom. If you bite and ravage each other, watch out—in no time at all you will be annihilating each other, and where will your precious freedom be then?

My counsel is this: Live freely, animated and motivated by God's Spirit. Then you won't feed the compulsions of selfishness. For there is a root of sinful self-interest in us that is at odds with a free spirit, just as the free spirit is incompatible with selfishness. These two ways of life are antithetical, so that you cannot live at times one way and at times another way according to how you feel on any given day. Why don't you choose to be led by the Spirit and so escape the erratic compulsions of a law-dominated existence?

It is obvious what kind of life develops out of trying to get your own way all the time: repetitive, loveless, cheap sex; a stinking accumulation of mental and emotional garbage; frenzied and joyless grabs for happiness; trinket gods; magic-show religion; paranoid loneliness; cutthroat competition; all-consuming-yet-never-satisfied wants; a brutal temper; an impotence to love or be loved; divided homes and divided lives; small-minded and lopsided pursuits; the vicious habit of depersonalizing everyone into a rival; uncontrolled and uncontrollable addictions; ugly parodies of community: I could go on.

This isn't the first time I have warned you, you know. If you use your freedom this way, you will not inherit God's kingdom.

But what happens when we live God's way? He brings gifts into our lives, much the same way that fruit appears in an orchard—things like affection for others, exuberance about life, serenity. We develop a willingness to stick with things, a sense of compassion in the heart, and a conviction that a basic holiness permeates things and people. We find ourselves involved in loyal commitments, not needing to force our way in life, able to marshal and direct our energies wisely.

Legalism is helpless in bringing this about; it only gets in the way: Among those who belong to Christ, everything connected with getting our own way and mindlessly responding to what everyone else calls necessities is killed off for good—crucified.

Since this is the kind of life we have chosen, the life of the Spirit, let us make sure that we do not just hold it as an idea in our heads or a sentiment in our hearts, but work out its implications in every detail of our lives. That means we will not compare ourselves with each other as if one of us were better and another worse. We have far more interesting things to do with our lives. Each of us is an original.

Nothing but the Cross

6 **Live creatively, friends.** If someone falls into sin, forgivingly restore him, saving your critical comments for yourself. You might be needing forgiveness before the day's out. Stoop down and reach out to those who are oppressed. Share their burdens, and so complete Christ's law. If you think you are too good for that, you are badly deceived.

Make a careful exploration of who you are and the work you have been given, and then sink yourself into that. Don't be impressed with yourself. Don't compare yourself with others. Each of you must take responsibility for doing the creative best you can with your own life.

Be very sure now, you who have been trained to a self-sufficient maturity, that you enter into a generous common life with those who have trained you, sharing all the good things that you have and experience.

Don't be misled: No one makes a fool of God. What a person plants, he will harvest. The person who plants selfishness, ignoring the needs of others—ignoring God!—harvests a crop of weeds. All he'll have to show for his life is weeds! But the one who plants in response to God, letting God's Spirit do the growth work in him, harvests a crop of real life, eternal life.

So let's not allow ourselves to get fatigued doing good. At the right time we will harvest a good crop if we don't give up, or quit. Right now, therefore, every time we get the chance, let us work for the benefit of all, starting with the people closest to us in the community of faith.

Now, in these last sentences, I want to emphasize in the bold scrawls of my personal handwriting the immense importance of what I have written to you. These people who are attempting to force the ways of circumcision on you have only one motive: They want an easy way to look good before others, lacking the courage to live by a faith that shares Christ's suffering and death. All their talk about the law is gas. They themselves don't keep the law! And they are highly selective in the laws they do observe. They only want you to be circumcised so they can boast of their success in recruiting you to their side. That is contemptible!

For my part, I am going to boast about nothing but the Cross of our Master, Jesus Christ. Because of that Cross, I have been crucified in relation to the world, set free from the stifling atmosphere of pleasing others and fitting into the little patterns that they dictate. Can't you see the central issue in all this? It is not what you and I do—submit to circumcision, reject circumcision. It is what God is doing, and he is creating something totally new, a free life! All who walk by this standard are the true Israel of God—his chosen people. Peace and mercy on them!

Quite frankly, I don't want to be bothered anymore by these disputes. I have far more important things to do—the serious living of this faith. I bear in my body scars from my service to Jesus.

May what our Master Jesus Christ gives freely be deeply and personally yours, my friends. Oh, yes!

Appendix

B CREDITS

World Harvest Mission is indebted to the following authors and publishers for permission to reprint excerpts from their copyrighted works:

Session 1 • p. 12
From *Knowing God* by J. I. Packer
Copyright © 1973, InterVarsity Press,
P.O. Box 1400, Downers Grove, IL 60515
(www.ivpress.com).
Used by permission.

Session 4 • pp. 63–67 • "The End of the Struggle"
From *Personal Revival* by Stanley Voke
Copyright © 1964, Operation Mobilization Literature.
Used by permission.

Session 7 • pp. 106–7 • "The Heart God Revives"
The Heart God Revives by Nancy Leigh DeMoss
Adapted from a message by Nancy Leigh DeMoss.
Copyright © Life Action Ministries,
P.O. Box 31, Buchanan, MI 49107-0031.
Used by permission.

Session 8 • pp. 121–22 • "What Is Faith?"
From *What Is Faith?* by Gresham Machen
Copyright © 1969, Wm B. Eerdmans Publishing Co.
Used by permission.

Session 9 • pp. 135–37 • "Sanctification"
From *Dynamics of Spiritual Life* by Richard F. Lovelace
Copyright © 1979, InterVarsity Press,
P.O. Box 1400, Downers Grove, IL 60515
(www.ivpress.com).
Used by permission.

Session 10 • pp. 151–52 • "The Rabbi's Heartbeat"
From *Abba's Child* by Brennan Manning
Copyright © 1994.
Used by permission of NavPress
(www.navpress.com).
All rights reserved.

Session 11 • pp. 165–67 • "The Great Sin"
From *Mere Christianity* by C. S. Lewis
Copyright © C. S. Lewis Pte. Ltd. 1942, 1943, 1944, 1952.
Extract reprinted by permission.

Session 12 • pp. 179–83 • "The Love of Christ Compels Us"
From *The Heart of a Servant Leader: Letters from Jack Miller*
by C. John Miller, ed. Barbara Miller Juliani, Copyright 2004.
Used by permission of P&R Publishing, Phillipsburg, NJ.

Session 13 • pp. 195–99 • "The Transforming Power of the Gospel"
"The transforming power of the gospel" by Steve Childers
Reformed Quarterly, Fall 1995.
Used by permission of Reformed Theological Seminary.

Session 14 • pp. 213–14 • "Daniel"
From *The Applause of Heaven* by Max Lucado
Copyright © 1996.
Used by permission of W Publishing Group, Nashville, TN.

Session 14 • pp. 216–23 • "Feeding Your Enemy"
"Feeding your Enemy" by Dan Allender
Discipleship Journal, Issue 71, 1992.
Used by permission of NavPress Publishing
(www.navpress.com).

Session 15 • pp. 238–43 • "Examine Yourself"

From *The Peacemaker* by Ken Sande
Copyright © 1991.
Used by permission of Baker Books, a division of Baker Book
House Company.

Appendix A • pp. 259–71 • The Book of Galatians

From *The Message*, The Scriptures translated
by Eugene Peterson
Copyright © by Eugene H. Peterson 1993, 1994, 1995.
Used by permission of NavPress Publishing Group.

MEMORY VERSES

SESSION

2

Thirsting for Righteousness

SESSION

4

Law and Gospel

SESSION

1

Orphans, or Children of God?

SESSION

3

Received Righteousness

Session 1: Orphans, or Children of God?

But when the time had fully come, God sent his Son, born of a woman, born under law, to redeem those under law, that we might receive the full rights of sons.

Galatians 4:4–5

Session 2: Thirsting for Righteousness

Because you are sons, God sent the Spirit of his Son into our hearts, the Spirit who calls out, "Abba, Father." So you are no longer a slave, but a son; and since you are a son, God has made you also an heir.

Galatians 4:6–7

Session 3: Received Righteousness

For in the gospel a righteousness from God is revealed, a righteousness that is by faith from first to last, just as it is written: "The righteous will live by faith."

Romans 1:17

Session 4: Law and Gospel

We know that the law is good if one uses it properly.

1 Timothy 1:8

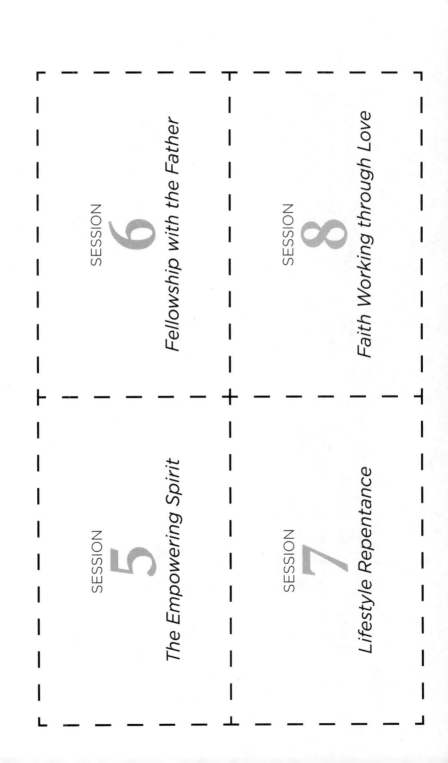

SESSION
5
The Empowering Spirit

SESSION
6
Fellowship with the Father

SESSION
7
Lifestyle Repentance

SESSION
8
Faith Working through Love

Session 6: Fellowship with the Father

"The LORD your God is with you, he is mighty to save. He will take great delight in you, he will quiet you with his love, he will rejoice over you with singing."

Zephaniah 3:17

Session 8: Faith Working through Love

For in Christ Jesus neither circumcision nor uncircumcision has any value. The only thing that counts is faith expressing itself through love.

Galatians 5:6

Session 5: The Empowering Spirit

May the God of hope fill you with all joy and peace as you trust in him, so that you may overflow with hope by the power of the Holy Spirit.

Romans 15:13

Session 7: Lifestyle Repentance

This is what the Sovereign LORD, the Holy One of Israel, says: "In repentance and rest is your salvation, in quietness and trust is your strength, but you would have none of it."

Isaiah 30:15

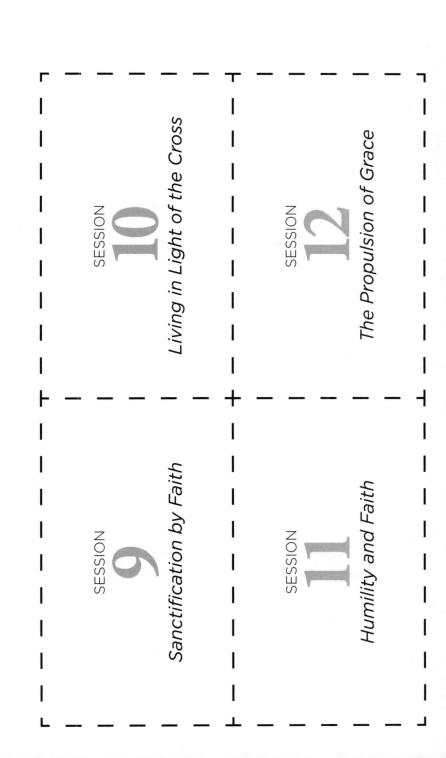

SESSION
9
Sanctification by Faith

SESSION
10
Living in Light of the Cross

SESSION
11
Humility and Faith

SESSION
12
The Propulsion of Grace

Session 9: Sanctification by Faith

Are you so foolish? After beginning with the Spirit, are you now trying to attain your goal by human effort? Have you suffered so much for nothing—if it really was for nothing? Does God give you his Spirit and work miracles among you because you observe the law, or because you believe what you heard?

Galatians 3:3–5

Session 10: Living in Light of the Cross

For the sinful nature desires what is contrary to the Spirit, and the Spirit what is contrary to the sinful nature. They are in conflict with each other, so that you do not do what you want.

Galatians 5:17

Session 11: Humility and Faith

But he gives us more grace. That is why Scripture says: "God opposes the proud but gives grace to the humble."

James 4:6

Session 12: The Propulsion of Grace

"But you will receive power when the Holy Spirit comes on you; and you will be my witnesses in Jerusalem, and in all Judea and Samaria, and to the ends of the earth."

Acts 1:8

SESSION

13

The Liberated Conscience

SESSION

14

Lifestyle Forgiveness

SESSION

15

Peacekeeping or Peacemaking?

SESSION

16

Weakness Evangelism

Session 13: The Liberated Conscience

How much more, then, will the blood of Christ, who through the eternal Spirit offered himself unblemished to God, cleanse our consciences from acts that lead to death, so that we may serve the living God!

Hebrews 9:14

Session 14: Lifestyle Forgiveness

Take words with you and return to the LORD. Say to him: "Forgive all our sins and receive us graciously, that we may offer the fruit of our lips."

Hosea 14:2

Session 15: Peacekeeping or Peacemaking?

"How can you say to your brother, 'Brother, let me take the speck out of your eye,' when you yourself fail to see the plank in your own eye? You hypocrite, first take the plank out of your eye, and then you will see clearly to remove the speck from your brother's eye."

Luke 6:42

Session 16: Weakness Evangelism

"So in everything, do to others what you would have them do to you, for this sums up the Law and the Prophets."

Matthew 7:12

mission
propelled by good news

At Serge we believe that mission begins through the gospel of Jesus Christ bringing God's grace into the lives of believers. This good news also sustains and empowers us to cross nations and cultures to bring the gospel of grace to those whom God is calling to himself.

As a cross-denominational, reformed, sending agency with more than 200 missionaries and 25 teams in 5 continents, we are always looking for people who are ready to take the next step in sharing Christ, through:

- **Short-term Teams**: One- to two-week trips oriented around serving overseas ministries while equipping the local church for mission

- **Internships:** Eight-week to nine-month opportunities to learn about missions through serving with our overseas ministry teams

- **Apprenticeships:** Intensive 12–24 month training and ministry opportunities for those discerning their call to cross-cultural ministry

- **Career:** One- to five-year appointments designed to nurture you for a lifetime of ministry

 Grace at the Fray   **Visit us online at: serge.org/mission**

spiritual
renewal
resources for you

Disciples who are motivated and empowered by grace to reach out to a broken world are handmade, not mass-produced. Serge intentionally grows disciples through curriculum, discipleship experiences, and training programs.

Resources for Every Stage of Growth

Serge offers grace-based, gospel-centered studies for every stage of the Christian journey. Every level of our materials focuses on essential aspects of how the Spirit transforms and motivates us through the gospel of Jesus Christ.

- **101**: The Gospel-Centered Series
  Gospel-centered studies on Christian growth, community, work, parenting, and more.

- **201**: The Gospel Transformation Series
  These studies go a step deeper into gospel transformation, involve homework and more in-depth Bible study

- **301**: The Sonship Course and Serge Individual Mentoring

Mentored Sonship

For more than 25 years Serge has been discipling ministry leaders around the world through our Sonship course to help them experience the freedom and joy of having the gospel transform every part of their lives. A personal discipler will help you apply what you are learning to the daily struggles and situations you face, as well as, model what a gospel-centered faith looks and feels like.

Discipler Training Course

Serge's Discipler Training Course helps you gain biblical understanding and practical wisdom you need to disciple others so they experience substantive, lasting growth in their lives. Available for onsite training or via distance learning, our training programs are ideal for ministry leaders, small group leaders or those seeking to grow in their ability to disciple effectively.

 Grace at the Fray   **Find more resources at serge.org**

www.newgrowthpress.com